# ARLINGTON WAY AND
# BISCUIT SHOES

# ARLINGTON WAY AND BISCUIT SHOES

FANNIE B. ERICKSON

**To order additional copies of this book, contact:**
Xlibris
1-888-795-4274
www.Xlibris.com
Orders@Xlibris.com
786605

By the Author:

The Blue Roof

Grandpa's Museum

Arlington Way and Biscuit Shoes

With gratitude to first draft readers:

Day Tait, Silver Quills member who dances with words.
Jeanne Pfeiffer, witty world traveler who taught English in Japan.
Paul Silva, Composition 101 and All-around Tech Guru.

# Foreword

A Mother's journal gives a subjective narration that deadpans the hilarious and the horrors of every day family life.

This read is fast. Agonizing heart felt revelations, unshakable beliefs, and panicked fears, blast through a whirl wind of raising kids and marriage in a mid-century industrial world.

Ahead of her time, she questioned a mill town's right to burn unused wood, 24/7, and describes (in Grandpa's Museum) the resulting pollution belching out of all those huge steel "tepees" in the 1950's.

Ahead of her time, she asked the Department of Motor Vehicles why a driving test must be done in a car, as opposed to a motorcycle, and why all the questions in the written test only related to driving a car, not a motorcycle. This inquiry, by the way, allowed a young apprentice motorcyclist to begin his lifelong passion. After all, she was the one to let go of the back of the bicycle, secretly, when she saw the stable speed wrapped around me. I still hear her no-nonsense voice, "Its b-i-c-y-c-l-e, that's how you spell it."

The manuscript for this book arrived with faint pencil markings. The author was asking me to mark where she "got it wrong."

I didn't mark a thing.

This book shows that in all the continuous fury of life, it all fits.

Steven

# One Mother's Day

"If you told me Mister died, Mother," she sobbed, "I would call in his ear so loud he would answer!" I wish death were that easy to explain but he is a dog and she is four.

The journal notes that began that way almost seven decades ago will end today. There is no use thinking I will not reread our family's younger years now that those musty pages have been uncovered in the cupboard below the book shelves. *And all you closed-mouth books are next to go!* in an attempt to downsize and organize for inevitable change. That box almost got added to my mountain of unnecessaries (polka dot ladders, an arthritic Underwood, a not-so-portable Singer, father and son's empty uniforms, a child's hand-print ashtray, who knows whose baby shoes and so on.). Heaven knows I appreciate the urgency to make a move, I most surely do, but the avalanche of decisions to distribute, donate, retain, or recycle has snowballed on me I fear.

After eighty-seven birthdays, though, what does an old woman actually need, or even want, really? Except sleep without dreams, a teacup and an oven door footstool, a book and a candle. *Jack be nimble, quick... and something about a candlestick? Let's write it down!* My mind, you see, hears voices. It wanders, disremembers, darts, slows, and at times just squats like a stubborn child in a baby harness.

It will be difficult reading cryptic scribblings about a once-lively family now that we can never all be together again. After the last child left this old house, the younger me innocently appended THE END to the journal. However, passing years, a stranger's correspondence, a brother's poignant poem, later letters and more current iPhone and eMail messages attest to a different ever after.

Pa always preferred his folks' little red Cedar Creek house an occasional weekend at a time instead of this foggy coast. Our eldest lives across the bridge; Pa had his seizure meds and said not to worry if his heart played out up there "so much the better." By the same token, if my faithful limbs do not lift me one more time, well then, the carpet here by the bookcase, my back against the wall, is as good a place as any if I can only reach... that... cushion. Better.

This time every year, the card dutifully arrives with four signatures, though one is a forgery bless their hearts. The children did not rearrange their schedules to be here this Mothers Day. I do not mind being alone; nothing to do, nowhere to go, no meals to prepare, suspenders to straighten, or socks to mate. I may read all day. The thing is, can I read dry-eyed past the days when we were all here. That's the thing, all those reminders of us.

Years ago, that dark-haired young wife, who prompts me nowadays, excitedly uprooted and planted me down two states from home and Mother, fully expecting me to thrive happily-ever-after in a strange environment beside a freeway at the top of California where the years quickly scooted past and earth-shattering events like first smiles, steps, shots or potty chair victories would be forgotten if not put to paper.

So the death of the first child's collie seemed important enough to be noted. It was our first serious conversation.

# Notebook

1951 Spring

"If you told me Mister died, Mother," Susan sobbed, "I would call in his ear so loud he would answer!" I wish death were that easy to explain but he is a dog and she is four.

Slobbery tears soaked my lap. She forgot sooner than I will, spent rest of day making mud pies sprinkled with Steven's baby powder.

At least future newspapers won't be delivered too dog-eared to read.

Our House: Shingle mill office, shabby add-on rooms under highway over-pass at dead end of Arlington Way alongside a slough, without a blade of grass.

My gangly, plane-crazy ex sailor invested savings from WW11 flight pay and sale of his Guadalcanal beer rations in his folks' small mill, intending to prove the need for an airplane. "We'll run three mills and I'll fly between," Richard fantasied.

Later. His high-flying plans not off the ground, still a millhand. This date is expected to last until death do its part, involves boss-parents-not-my-own, more labor, too late to strike, protest, or picket.

Blond Peggy Lee sings in radio on window sill overlooking smelly log pond Is This all There is? Kids nap, I wail along with her, make out millhands' time cards, plan dinner, write Mother.

A Saturday. Susan, Steven, I, listen to radio, Wild Bill Hickock. They're perched on drainboard. We crack a big fifty-cent crab. Susan's arm around Steven.

He's fussy not being held. Richard: "Enjoy it. That's what you wanted, right?"

Right. To keep me company when his mother takes Susan up to Cedar Creek for company. And to avoid typing at big Dolly Varden Lumber Mill next door when Susan starts school.

One evening. Susan pushed water away at dinner table, "No, I won't drink it!" She ate, eyes closed. I explain radio program, blind girl. Richard says oh, returns her glass.

Today Susan reads Casper Ghost funny book, making it up as she goes. Steven, I, listen to Saturday at the Opera series. He wrinkles nose at soprano's high notes, laughs at everything sister does. She sneezes, he giggles until hiccups. She asks if all boys are that silly.

Steven, 6 mo., still demanding night bottle. What with one thing and another, I'm tired, sleepy all day.

Susan at Granny's again. No chattering, "Where's my dog leash?" "Put on my Gene Autry record, please." An Only raised with five adults, Richard doesn't speak Children. He's learning.

Says it's easy to be impatient with kids but let them be gone one hour and, damn, you go nuts.

If she comes back with more new toys I might. No room for another Madame Alexander Little Women doll from Safeway or another new outfit I cannot afford.

Another foggy Sunday.
Tired from working two shifts all week, anything we said or did set Richard off. He lists what should or shouldn't be done, speeds off, car spitting dusty gravel.

I open oil valve in heater stove, forget, blow stove pipe apart when puddle finally lights! Soot rains on cretonne curtains, blue curly mohair sofa from home, the children.

Mop up before He returns. Susan still hiding in bedroom with Steven, their racoon-eye makeup repaired.

"Lit the stove again didja' Gertrude?" Fat Gertrude or skinny Emma; I answer to neither. His mood is improved, mine isn't. He takes Susan's hand, tells me to get the baby, wants to show me something, "But you really should look in the mirror first."

Open House Models. New Sunny Brae Subdivision.
His level driveway, my blue kitchen, three bedrooms, automatic furnace. Ticky-tacky boxes all in a row to Beat poets, mansions to us. Pioneer $9,000, Frontier $11,000, Westerner $15,000.

Richard dreams far too big for me. Wants his private pilot's license, new car, better job, a Westerner.

No fun dealing with his resentment about work, where we live, inability to get into aviation, the cold Model A. Automatic furnace would be nice, though.

La-a-a-ter. Some of Richard's day dreams become real. Got pilot's license on G.I. Bill, paid off new Buick in nine months learning to saw shingles two shifts a day and all but one inch of his left wrist.

Month's stay in hospital. Nurse's photo in billfold when he returns. Said he didn't know.

Three-mill fantasy takes a nose dive. We put returned investment down on next Westerner. Richard readily agrees no new car til house is paid off, forgetting thirty-year mortgage.

Now, hauling lumber from Cedar Creek Mill, more to his liking. Pretends lumber is turned sideways and he's flying down off Berry Summit.

Before move, Susan, 5, falls in slough. Rusty cans, broken bottles, dead dogs, racoons. Who knows what else? Top of head dry, that deep. I spank her til Richard stops me. She stays near him rest of day.

Waiting for FHA loan. Richard modernizing his baby chests, building coffee table, we practice drinking.

Will move with two but what with one thing and another, third baby due next year.

1952. August 9, Susan's 6th birthday. New car, new house, soon, new baby. Eating lots of five-cent eggs. Richard asks what's for dinner, I say breakfast.

Our own New House.
We sit on grass, wait for Daddy with beds in borrowed mill truck. New neighbor asks about my little brother and sister. I get up. Never mind looking too young, don't want to act it.

Susan starts school. Half days. Classroom shortage. Teacher says, "I seen..." Teacher shortage, too?

Took her picture on driveway. Navy Chesterfield coat, Mary Janes, leaning to kiss Steven in stroller, waving to us.

No waiting alone for school bus on highway, no hoboes sleeping behind tepee burner, no putrid ponds, logs swinging over house, railroad beside slough.

Susan. Two vaccinations. Rubbed first off on wall. Says she'd rather have the disease than be shot.

I money-worry. Now need garbage can, drapes, lawn mower, fence. Richard says he doesn't drink, gamble, or chase women, so he should be able to buy something for house once in a while.
After Christmas cheer at work he fumbles wrapping on handsome brass mailbox. "Don't gamble, don't drink, so I should be able to..."

Steady diet of scrambled eggs. R. says tooth fairy will probably lay one. Susan heard.

Notes for Granny when I go to hospital: Steven, 18 months, Susan, 7. Steven wakes at 8:00. Breakfast: toast, little pig sausages in hand, milk. If busy, give him orange wedge. Likes soggy cold cereal, ick. And pancakes in hand. Warning. He sticks fingers in butter. Will nap when Susan leaves for school at 11:00.

He wants bankey with satin binding, while he sucks two middle fingers, like Susan. Baby food while dinner cooks. In play pen when you eat, Susan entertains him in pen.

1953. March 28. New Baby. David born at nine.
After coffee, paper, cigarette, Richard drops me off at hospital on way to work, promises to give us a ride home if he remembers. Not amusing when pain involved, mainly mine.

"You predicted a girl this time!" I accuse doctor.

"This says, 'Erickson, boy,'" he grins, holds out little black book, flaps it shut, leaves.

Nurse-friend winks. Said if mother disputes Doc, he opens book where he wrote opposite of what he told her originally. "Don't let on I said anything." She leaves, arms full, kicks door closed, I nap.

Home three days later, not ten days like first birth that left tingling feet. Neighbors' maternity shower favored a girl. David sleeps well in pink.

Took no time getting used to Steven's little round face like picture in Good Housekeeping Baby Book.

Took even less time bonding with David's long face like Daddy, lighter hair like Susan, her pouty rosebud lips. He's a sweetie. Steven says, "Hi Teedie."

Steven, too lively at times but hugs from dimpled little arms and he's easier to take. My arms too baby-busy with David, Steven misses holding, rocking.

Steven speaks his own language. Kickin', for kitchen. Hep cub up, for help me cover up. Reen, for rain. Fambly, for family. Bahboo, for bathroom, which serves no purpose until he learns to remove his pants. Says same thing for thank you, confusing even himself.

Home from work, Richard hands him domed lunch pail, shakes hands, "How do you do, Steven?" who turns to shake Susan's, says, "Hi, Do." Her nickname.

Door bell rings. Steven says bahboo, is aimed there immediately. I answer door while loudly reminding Steven, "Take off your pants!"

Open door to mail at my feet, glimpse mailman quickly headed out driveway, without postage due.

Dinner. Susan eats prawns, refuses Brussels sprouts, gags, influencing Steven. If Do won't eat sprouts, he won't. She dries dishes, grumbling,

"Boy, if you don't like one thing, they give you two things you don't like. No Fair!"

Between three children, new puppy Granny thinks we need, will lose David's baby fat. Been leaning backward, top-heavy this time. First time up, toppled over.

Two weeks to work new baby into family sleep, eat, play, bathe routine, then pink plaid sweater-dress will fit.

Granny gifts new dress each baby, hopes for nine grandchildren. Plan to limit her hopes and my wardrobe.

Gift for Susan's birth was wrap-around maternity dress, first one in stores. Steven's "after baby" dress was sleeveless blue-green paper nylon, full net half-slips underneath. Granny thinks I'm still eighteen.

After Sunday School Susan helps give away Granny's collie puppies. One man likes police dogs. Susan: "This is their secret service uniform. They're really German Shepherds."

To read when I'm old:
Baby David in crib, Steven locked in highchair, Susan in pjs. Make exaggerated show unfolding, placing paper napkin in lap. Steven puts his in milk glass, then wears it like a collar. Susan bites tongue, uses hers, screams, likes when it bleeds, shows Steven who doesn't.

She was too hungry to wait for breakfast, now has chairs in row for train game, French toast cools. Steven puts leftovers in glass, stirs, shows Susan who yells yuck, he giggles. They wake David. So much for leisurely breakfast.

Every night two a.m., David makes squeaky-toy noise, hides face while I cup my hand on his stomach, sounds like a hollow pumpkin. He turns over to get bottom patted. "Now you go to sleep, right now, Little Punkin!"

He giggles, wiggles fat little feet. Not hungry, just likes the game. How long does this go on?

Steven gives David little red Christmas ball. We count pieces, call doctor, feed soft bread, play dreadful waiting game til tiny curved red sliver bites his bottom.

New rule: No feeding baby through crib bars, Pulled first grey hair.

Started for church. Susan screamed, something wrong with Steven, eyes rolled up. Got him to my lap, held tongue down, teeth clamping middle finger, yell for Richard to turn for hospital Now!

Steven had fever and I didn't know? Some children can't tolerate even small fever, but outgrow it. Tiny teeth marks will remind me.

Richard gets out of once-yearly church service.

Coffee times, rare:
Baby David fed, in crib, playing. Susan, Steven, quiet in front room with Christmas Stories. Buttered muffin, went for coffee. Returned as Susan left with half. Got cream, Steven walked away with other half then returned for my magazine.

Someday, lots of time for coffee, reading, sleeping.

Susan screamed, "Steven, let go of baby!" I called. He came dragging David by one leg like Susan's Pitiful Pearl doll, bumped baby across kitchen door sill. David cries.

Steven stoops, tries to kiss back of brother's head, looks up, "What now you want for me."

Steven, 3, burned finger on my iron. Called Susan to entertain him. She fell off trike, skinned knee. She moaned, he howled, they woke David, usually a happy napper, noise scared him.

Ironing not finished, supper not ready, felt good to rock, cry along with all three. Daddy arrives, yells, "So, how was your day, Emma?"

A Saturday. Richard wanted restaurant breakfast. The works, no hurrying. "Let's read the paper, then get dressed. Okay?"

Check children, slip them cereal, juice, funnies, dare them to leave room on pain of death. Dressed, well fed, they want outside with favorite neighbor.

Barry goes window to window jumping like a yo yo to see in. He handily fills the unfortunate five-year age gap between Do and Steven.

Finally in kitchen, Richard says, "See, the kids don't gobble. They're being nice and quiet." Of course they are!

Their untouched plates my buffet. Never saw paper and He thinks we should have more nice Saturdays like that.

A too-busy day.
Didn't know if I was coming or going. Susan: "Me too! I was upside down, I didn't know whether to go or leave." She's got to be mostly Dutch from His side.

Baby David, toothless 9 mo. Now, two uppers, two lowers. Scarce of hair also. Richard carries him through Ten-Cent store wearing doll's wig and price tag which I had to return.

David tries to stand alone, too bottom-heavy, sweet, cuddly. Leans head on mine, coos softly, "Ohh."

Barry's mother, best-friend-Mildred and I perch him on kitchen table between us, like a big doll. He Ohhs both of us, tries to sip our coffee.

David has ear infection. Ear drum broke. Penicillin shots. Left ear.

Now, Steven. Right ear. Impetigo on chin irritated by orange juice and a bad mother.

Went to town. Looked at M.G.s. Any time Richard spots one, follows it for blocks. This is no country for little English convertibles.

1954. January. Richard took Greyhound bus to San Francisco. Drove new M.G., $2,000, home 40 mph, arrives 4:00 a.m. Got me out of bed, rode around block in nightgown, barefoot.

David has two stitches on forehead. At sink washing hands, he pulled, I impatiently pushed at wrong time. My fault. He cried, I cried, Doctor's son, in office to watch, learn. He cried.

Summer 1954. Ten-year high school reunion. Excuse to go home.

Didn't go. Richard grudgingly let one neighbor drive new M.G. Something amiss with ring gear.
Tearing it down, staying up nights. I put on new dress, forties records, sad face, sit in lady chair, listen to Boogie Woogie, Marie, Star Eyes, Stardust, feel sorry for myself, He doesn't notice.

Fire in Front Room!
Throw-rug over magazine rack catches fire, burns three fireplace panel boards, yard of carpet. Throw Navy blanket on fire, He throws water on me.

Had been discussing future, kitchen door closed. Should we move? No winter work, mills closed, long lines at unemployment office. Smoke in children's rooms!

Insurance adjuster, clipboard in hand, "Now, tell me, was this a friendly fire or hostile fire?"

Phone installed.

Never get to talk. Today, push David, in only his undershirt, toward bahboo, he detours out in rain. Motion Steven to get brother.

Steven joins him in gushing gutter. Drop phone mid-sentence, pull both in, David blue-bottomed, Steven, sopping wet, shoes and all. Neighbors are entertained, saw curtains twitch.

Love Stevens mischievous giggle, David's juicy laugh.

Susan sick. Missed Hawaiian Day at school. Today I painted kitchen. Every item from walls is on kitchen table. Tonight, we eat with fingers, Daddy objects to sitting on floor, under table, eating fruit, rice, on poison lily leaves, refuses to wear lei.

Got blonde GE TV, black iron stand. Richard will build it into front room closet. Neighbor children gather on stomachs, watch Dobbie Gillis, Gilligan's Island.

August 9. Flew home. New grey shantung, red heels, purse. Susan, nylon dress, redingote to match, from Granny. Sat across isle with gentleman not pleased.

She hooked bird toy on curtain, squeezed bulb making it tweet, flap wings. Closed and opened curtain while man tried to read official-looking papers. Couldn't reach her. Pretends she can't read my pursed lips, crossed eyes.

David on my lap, buckled Steven in, seat belt locked. He found combination - b-a-h-b-o-o. Three of us in a one-seater.

After a week, Richard came, drove us home. What with one thing and another, fourth baby due next year.

Another little girl would make all our worries, job, money, moving if we have to, seem small. Only sewing pink. With crossed fingers.

1955. March, 28. David's birthday, 2. Tiny red wagon. Steven pulls him.

April 3, 1955. Linda born.
Perfectly comfortable this time while Catholic Sister-nurse is up to her wrist manually monitoring centimeter progress while we have nice long conversation, oblivious, all modesty spent. At birth of the first-born, tried to close my knees. In stirrups. Nurse quipped "too late."

When Richard, Granny approach, nurse-friend warns, I feign sleep. When doc approaches, I warn her off my bed, float on air of satisfaction. A girl.

Doc brings med students. I ask nurse what "three pears or piece of watermelon" means. She was sure he must have said "repairs or episiotomy," shook her head at my ignorance.

She hands me another obnoxious cocktail to ensure bottle feeding, kernels under my arms, nobody warned me about that. And chin-tweezing for the rest of my life.

Granny's after-baby dress gift is long-waisted beige Lass O'Scotland nubby knit from Dalys Department Store, below knee, size 10.

Two-month-old Linda laughs aloud when jiggled on knee. Gas? Got hiccups, went to sleep. Neighbors showered pink for David, this time, blue. She doesn't care.

Now Richard says, "Two boys, two girls, no more, enough is four!" Doctor explains a solution but he is Catholic.

Doctor of a different persuasion looks both ways, lets Richard in and out back door on a Saturday. Better him than me, less serious, less money.

Mother writes, "You have fulfilled your purpose in life, replaced yourselves and multiplied." I feel better.

Economy down. Neighbors circulate recipe for one-egg cake, cook economical fish sticks, drink Tang, eat tuna casserole, make Jello-fruit cocktail, use hamburger helper one hundred ways, save enough left-overs all week for Friday minestrone. Monsodium glutimate on everything.

Trucker's wife, end of block, considers limiting toilet tissue to two sheets, she states on bridge nite.

House payments keep increasing, started at $60, Four per cent interest, thirty years.

Training David. One neighbor makes sure our boys stay playtime dry. At her house they go bahboo every half hour, no water-drinking. Her son at our house, ditto.

Little boys think stop-watch mothers are as much nuisance as button-front coveralls.

1956. Richard finally in AVIATION!
We think he's Lindbergh. He *GETS* to polish planes at airport in Eureka, clean public toilets, set fence posts on owner's ranch, $1.00 hour. After FAA test will make $2.45 hr.

Has Aviation Maintenance Engineer on back of button-front coveralls, which he also thinks are a nuisance.

Showed up at airport every day asking for work, frustrated owner threatened police, swearing involved. Richard promised not to return for two weeks. Owner calls foreman, "Find something for this guy to do for God sakes, he's not going to give up!"

He takes small bouquets in fruit jars for public toilets. Garages little M.G. under wide wing airplane, avoids rent.

Linda poses for picture standing by sofa with Susan ready to catch. Other three walked thirteenth mo. Slow her down, simplify record keeping.

Hide $20 mo. under ask-it basket on top of Fridgedaire. If not spent for food end of pay period, it goes in bank.

Dining out, Chinese restaurant, Grandpa treats. First time out with all four, last time out until all are twenty-four!

Susan got to order from menu, David played cars with crackers, Linda squirmed, Steven said his teeth hurt, cried. Steven, Linda, I, left, waited in Buick. We were not missed.

Steven, David play house with girl, four, from across street:
She says, "See, you say 'What you doin', Momma?'" When boys say that, she answers, then tells them next thing to say. She's upset; Steven won't call her "Momma."

Momma hangs from swing by her knees, her Fruit of the Looms on display, bare chested, dress hiding head, yells to boys, "You can't be the Momma, 'cause I act like a Momma!"

She leaves, boys resume game, then quit, neither wants to be a Momma 'cause they have to yell on people.

1958. Got driver's license at 28.
Took all four children and Granny, to entertain DMV personnel. At last minute, changed to red heels.

Mentally dare examiner to require parking. He kindly explains how to approach stop street, when to signal, pull-out, position foot over brake, says don't be nervous, doesn't require parking. I swear to drive only when necessary, never to pass, never to park.

David swallows penny!

Gasps, turns red, blue. Got kids in car to hospital. Receptionist says sit, fill out form, wait your turn. David chokes, coughs, throws up.

ARLINGTON WAY AND BISCUIT SHOES

I wipe his face, he breathes long breaths, smiles sweetly, we leave, tip on floor. Woman waves unfinished form.

Took children, and Susan's best friend with us, to dentist. Elevator went on up as Susan approached button. "But - but - was it something I said?" Friend thinks Susan is hilarious, Susan thinks friend is too serious, she makes A in every subject.

Girls take Linda out, bring her back white-faced, blue lipped, tell me Linda likes elevators.

Carry Linda to car. Steven, David turn right, under swinging bar doors next to Hollander's Jewelry store.

Pretend no one sees red-faced Sunday School teacher struggling out of beer hall carrying one child, leading two more, Susan and friend too far ahead for help.

Left car before alley to get out. Find old red pickup squeezed in front of Buick. Six tries forward, back, back and forth, wrench big steering wheel, wipe brow, tell kids to stop counting, Shut Up, pull out.

Mechanics, lunching in garage across street, applaud. Their pickup.

Susan says kleptomaniac set house on fire. I explain, she responds "He stole the matches."

She is ironing too, with her little warm iron, all her ribbons, the skirt she has on, Linda's stuffed cat. Linda screams.

Linda, David weekly grocery-shop with me, David in Barry's welcome hand-me-overs, Linda wears organdy Sunday dress from twins down the street, high top white shoes.

On Plaza, in old store with wooden floors, David waits at tall candy bar display, follows us to car carrying giant Hershey bar long as his arm.

Tells me a lady asked him what he wanted "and that's what I wanted." Tried not to smile after he returned it. So did he.

David brought new friend in to meet me, without knocking, while I bathed. Grabbed bath mat, "His coveralls are just like yours, David." "He'th a girl, thilly." They left, door open.

Late fixing dinner. Steven learning to count, got to fourteen, got impatient, sent him to bedroom. He opened door, yelled "fifteen, sixteen!" Slammed it.

Is learning to write instead of print, thought I should know that too, opened door again, "And you can write that in your little old note book and don't print it!"

He was angry, I was worse, cackled I would boil him in oil if he kept bothering me, worse than the witch in Oz. He hates her. The others joined him in bedroom. Neither he nor they said much at dinner. Bad Mother. Dr. Spock would not approve.

Answered phone question, won dance lesson from Arthur Murray studio, two couples. Mildred and I begged husbands who agreed just to shut us up.

Young redheaded instructor, wearing knit jumper bare to waist under arms, only danced tango with husbands, told us to go practice.

Mildred and I did not fit together, largely her fault. We laughed against wall, legs crossed.

Her husband signed for $65 lessons before he knew what happened.

Last night, Barry, stayed all night. Tells us this a.m. that every time we put David back to bed he said, "I don't like Mother, she stinks, I don't like my Daddy, he stinks. Now, he says Barry stinks, too.

Susan named broom for favorite horse book, does not offer to sweep, hands me the reins, "You can use My Friend Flicka." She snorts, whinnies, gallops around the house with friend also besotted with horses.

White chimney has black horse Daddy cut out of tin, coffee table now has tile horse in center which Susan completed. Rest of us tiled background. All in lieu of a live one.

Sunday, church. David caught a sunbeam in his hand during silent prayer, loudly announced, "Oh boy, the thun ith out!" Congregation laughs, he claps.

Granny dresses Susan in Lana Turner sweater, pearls, at her house. I braid pig tails, just because. She dislikes them.

Yesterday. David brought little friend for lunch. Elbows on table, chin in hands, said he already had lunch. When asked what, said, "Breakfast. My Mom sleeps late." Lucky her.

Today, that recent divorcee planned to fly out of town with man friend for lunch. Her three youngest children were in our yard watching me paint our house. She yelled across she'd be back before dinner, asked could her children play with mine til then, left. I'm not a fast thinker. Lucky her.

Today boys made hole through wall in their closet to spy on girls. Linda, furious. Daddy, too. We started swear cup.

Linda impatiently sits through 40s records, asks me to put her long-play record on cabinet radio, leaves to play. Mildred comes over, finds me ironing, we tango to Puff and Toot.

Bank account $3,375.00.

Drive-in movie. Children bathe, get on pajamas, make popcorn, take Pepsi treat. All asleep before we get home. Ali Baba and the forty thieves, jugs of oil.

Bargain hunting after Christmas with $20. Got Linda a tricycle, set of Melmac dishes to save rooster ones for best, David, new tennis shoes, tires for his little red bike, formerly Barry's.

Mildred asks about Linda's teeth thru chin when she rode trike off two steps to garage. She is fine, had just spilled puddle of homemade pink shoe polish for Susan's shoes. I go for coffee pot.

Mildred picks up dauber, finishes chore from puddle on floor. Six pair Sunday shoes on Formica kitchen table. We take picture.

Treasures:
-Susan hides chocolate, pencils, broken glider, ceramic Lassie, behind furnace door in hall.
-Steven treasures paper baseball hat he sleeps in, that came with house paint, comb that came with flea collar. Another Christmas cat dumped off in Sunny Brae.
-David's sheet-covered springs under mattress every pocket filled with rocks, tiny water bottle.
-Linda's hidey place is doll buggy. Took cancelled checks, left my Chanel No. 5.

Stormy night. Turn to edge of bed, lightening, two brown eyes large as a Keane painting level with mine.

Thunder rumbles, Linda says hi, crawls over me to middle, takes half my pillow, likes covers down, arms out, sleeps on her back, legs spread eagle, doesn't know when Daddy takes her out his side back to her bed.

Tonight. Told boys to stop playing, finish dinner. Linda says, "An you better do what the mean old giant says or she'll put you to bed!"

Good excuse to put her there, early, with Teddy bear, grumbling under my breath, "That's enough of you for today, little missy!" so she couldn't hear.

Teddy hit the floor before my feet reached the door. "NUFFA YOU today, Bear!" she says so I can hear.

Annoying Word Games. Each takes a turn:
-White, white, you got married in a thewer pipe.
-See my thumb? Gee, you're dumb.
-Fatty, fatty, two by four, can't get through the kicken door.
-Green, green you're no queen. Stick your head in gasolene.
-Red, red, you wet the bed.
-Yellow, yellow, you kithed a fellow
-Black, black, you sat on a tack, rolling down the railroad track.
-Blue, blue, you got the flu, not going to play with you.
-Look, look, rubber neck, ten cents a stretch.

Steven promised to give David two black horses and one red wagon. That was a nice thing to say. "Oh, yeah? That means two black eyes and a bloody nose!"

Mean old giant. Those Teddy bears are sickly, scruffy, unsanitary, balding, show signs of having been fed more oatmeal than their owners ate, and I can't get rid of them!

Children yelled in unison when they saw a leg sticking out of garbage can, rescued them.

Board games bore me. Monopoly is played in dining room on picnic table. Game lasts three days. Barry plays. Richard gets involved. He cheats.

Kids haven't missed the bears. Yet. They were whisked away garbage day in Daddy's little old Navy suitcase. He bot luggage and hitchhiked one thousand miles home! "Yeah," he says, proudly. "But I saved bus fare and I still have the suitcase." Not anymore.

Do Teddy bears get claustrophobia? Because I'm having trouble breathing.

Parent Teacher conference:
-Steven making steady progress in everything.
-David not doing his best. Is bored. "I've done that already."
-Do does what she's supposed to. No problems, nothing to report.

Susan babysat Barry Friday for $2.00. Mowed elderly neighbor's lawn for 50 cents. Won't again. He snapped elastic waistband on her pedal pushers.

Hemmed black chiffon dress for oldest neighbor's next "shindig." Ten yards around, $4.00 and pumpkin pie payment. Hand rolled. Impossible on old Singer.

Airport. Richard flies to repair planes. Has Aircraft and Engine license, $2.45 hr. Flew company pilot to pick up seed and plane to finish a job today. Commercial pilot left plane, rode bus home yesterday, fog.

1959. RICHARD LOST IN FOG.
He flew under fog down coast to fix County Aviation Director's plane. Director stayed overnight. Richard couldn't afford to, tried to get home. Fog closed in.

Fellow mechanic arrived to tell us just as TV newscaster announced "Erickson was last seen headed out to sea."

At that moment Richard opened front door, face white enough to show every whisker, told us about two trees he banked plane between after looking down to see why people were lying on a dock.

He landed on beach without hitting a log or bending a strut, climbed a metal fence, ran from a dog, found a phone, asked where he was, thought he was 90 miles north in Crescent City.

He could call, could not receive on defective radio in company's stripped-down Cessna. Will be remembered for yelling at the tower, "If you can't hear me, dammit, tell me!"

Linda Gets Lost Too! Missing two hours.
Mildred, Linda and I finished tuna sandwiches on patio. Linda, sleepy, was sent in for nap while we cleared table. Came in to empty house. Yard, neighborhood searched. Neighbors helped.

Notified radio station, "Three year old female, wearing yellow bathing suit and sandals missing in Sunny Brae subdivision."

Oldest neighbor, 60, circling in car, spotted Linda four houses away looking out picture window. Owner works. Linda followed cat down street, fell asleep on neighbor's bed.

Mechanic from Norway came to work at airport. Brings lunch with crackers, cheese, fish, snacks. Richard wants cracker snacks, too, with Limburger cheese. A different sandwich every day wasn't difficult enough? Now kids want stinky snacks.

Sold swing set, crib, for $7.00 each. Sad. Neighbor says, "When you are all through with children's things, it is sad," shakes her grey head, "but life has to move along." Next day, hennaed her hair.

Took Susan and Steven to see Carousel recently.

This week took them to see Music Man movie. Steven eagerly explains to Daddy how the rag-taggle music students suddenly turned into professional band, beautiful uniforms, polished instruments. "See, that's how it seemed to the band leader and he made everyone believe."

Kids switch words the way Daddy does. David may say his knot has a shoestring in it, Steven, his shiny is really apple. They imitate when he switches first letters, like, "You are loo tate." And his habit of calling everything gravy. Mayonaise, catsup, salad dressing. They'll crazy me drive.

Report card day. Steven's weakest point is reading comprehension. Richard says he has a hard time reading that big word, too. Children laugh. He's no help.

Boy who walks home with David keeps pushing, hitting. David is going to pick up a rock and thock him. Steven says, "No, no! A rock is harmier, just hit or push him and it will stop hurting later. A rock lasts a long time!"

Steven tells David his history lesson. "See, Hammer Lincoln lived in a login house and walked 14 miles to get a book. Bet you didn't know that."

Barry ran down hill out of breath, "Steven's on top of the water tower!" Both jumped down onto tank but crossing that space uphill stumped Steven. Went up there, told him to come down here This Minute.

Steven tells Barry, "Boy! When Mother tells you to do something, you do it!"

Sad day for Susan. Found another home for her black and white collie.

Kids continually leave backyard gate open, Mildred mentions dog barking, neighbors report difficulty with newly-planted lawns, postman threatens to stop delivery. Had to face facts, hide them from Susan, Granny.

Farm family arrived as Susan came from school. Colleen would not get in truck. Susan snapped her fingers, the dog trusted her. No crying. Not then.

Richard critical all through breakfast, upsetting everyone. Grandpa had made a disparaging remark about Richard owning a sports car. Richard put his MG for sale on local radio program.

When he left, I ask children what they wanted to do for fun after school:
-Susan thinks most fun is just getting out of school.
-Steven wants a towel cape to play Zorro. Thinks an old sheet would be even gooder.
-David wants to watch cement truck pour a driveway, eat outside on patio, and just "do stuff."
-Linda wants to play with her friend across the street in one of Susan's dresses. Uh oh.

Took ad off the air for M.G. Richard works hard, doesn't borrow money, and Granny and Grandpa are no longer our boss.

Sunday. Susan bought Richard candy and key ring for Fathers day. Went for ride, each kid had two ice creams.

Thought things went well in back seat. Heard later about David's need for empty bottle. He carries tiny water bottle in pocket, Steven told him to drink it then use it. We return with cones, newspaper. Kids are yelling.
Susan, "I'm tellin'!"
Steven, "Stop, David!"
David, "I can't!"

Gave Susan a home Toni permanent, turns light brown hair lighter, looks like Shirley Temple. Smells.

Today, beds made, everybody dressed before breakfast. Dishes, floors done in time for I Love Lucy on TV at ten.

Hard to keep kids entertained during summer. Started reading Tom Sawyer to them, Barry, and raspberry neighbor's son, on the lawn. They wander off one at a time except Barry.

We went for walk to Baywood Golf Course, kids dragging sticks behind them in middle of gravel road.

Committed to teach summer church school. Susan led children's games, Steven wore Richard's robe, carried dates in pocket for one story. David, Linda liked snacks. Used up two weeks of summer.

Susan and A-student friend go with Steven to sell mistletoe gathered from Berry Summit oaks Thanksgiving at Granny's. Friend doesn't sell because it would reflect on her accountant father. Susan says friend is missing fun money.

Steven, David sell some of Granny's small Christmas trees in our front yard. Steven also sells popcorn in small baggies at school ball games. Has bank book. David banks in dresser drawer.

Linda still has trouble keeping shoes on; clothes, no better. Used to strip, walk around with her clothes in bag. Neighbor found complete outfit on her stoop, guessed the owner. Owner's next present is a small suitcase.

Susan wears blue jeans with Mary Janes, crinolines with black tennis shoes. Thought boy craze had gotten her.

Its Tony this, Tony that. "I think he likes me. I hate brown bread and baloney so I give him mine." The stray dog hangs around school mooching lunches.

Boys throw pair of rolled-up socks to far corner of back yard, order Linda to fetch! until she is dog-tired. Encourage her to crawl thru pipe under Golf Course road when they wouldn't!

Linda fell, scraped lip, held head back to stop bleeding. With thick lip, imitates Alfred Hitchcock, hums his TV theme holding her head copying his thick-lip silhouette. Steven doesn't like the blood but thinks she's funny, urges her to do it again, calls Daddy to watch.

Sunday. Richard worked six weeks without a day off. We washed Buick so he wouldn't be critical, mowed lawn so he wouldn't say everything was going to pot, fixed dinner early so he wouldn't get a headache.

Susan went on picnic with girlfriends. Came home with pop and chips, her money. Even though it was after dinner we had a party. Said she felt bad about leaving me today. Now, everyone is back to bed. Have just finished cleaning kitchen. Again. Happy Mothers Day to me.

New mower. Sort of. Richard put washing machine motor on the push one. Children wonder why ours sounds like a B-24.

Now David cannot turn it over to race with neighbor twins clacking down middle of our street.

Sunday. Susan was left home first time when family went for ride. She promised to set table, time roast in oven. Rubbed it with every spice in cupboard, even cinnamon, cloves.

For years, chicken, chocolate cake on Sunday. Now we like spiced roast beef, white cake on picnic table in front of TV.

Wizard of Oz movie after dinner. Steven to his room til witch goes away.

We have twenty-four pottery bowls with handles, from car rides. Box of four when we gas up at Richfield. Children like them for popcorn, ice cream, chili.

Also crown-shaped bottle Prince Matchabelli perfume from car dealer's opening, and $25.00 E Bond for test driving new car we can't afford.

County Fair. Took children, Barry. All got headaches, bumps, nausea, from rides. All agreed Best Day Ever.

Susan, out of mood for church. Daddy lectures she is lucky to have nice house, sister, brothers who are well, good health, and if she can't at least make an appearance on Sunday as a show of thanks she doesn't deserve them. She went, wondered why he didn't.

David and Linda have tonsils out, can have unlimited ice cream, even that hurts. Gave them each a silver Cessna earring to take.

Would have scrubbed floors like Irene Dunne in movie Mama's Bank Account to be near them. Neither earring made it home.

After another Saturday helping Granny, Grandpa at Cedar Creek, Barry, too. Kids impatient to head home. Richard let them start walking dirt road to hiway.

Car packed, caught them half mile down 299, single file, Barry leading, Steven, then David, and Linda trying to keep ahead of Susan bringing up rear. On wrong side of highway.

Ringworm. Boys still have to wear Richard's sailor hats with principal's permission. New friend on block took in stray cat that soon had kittens. Found scaly spot on Steven's neckline, doctor prescribed terrible purple stain.

Shaving his head, washing it every day in laundry tray did not save David whose case is severe.

Now David's best friend needs a sailor hat.

Made cone covers, dunce caps, they say, to wear at night. They yell ringworm! at sailors on TV. No cure in sight. Thankfully, girls are spared.

Dentist trip. Took Linda in by dental chair with me so David wouldn't tease. She lay on floor coloring, told Dr. Brown she had no supper last night, while she scratched Donald Duck with green crayon. Small town. Had to explain.

David developed a fibroma from biting his lip during lectures for being late for dinner. Last night family looked for him and Linda while food cooled. Gave them bread and milk, sent them to bed like Hansel and Gretel.

Richard asked David how he would feel if we made him worry like that.

David wanted to see where water went when man turned fire hydrant on, followed it down the gutter, showed Linda the seven-redwood tree fort in the woods.

Richard says he is going with them next time. I frowned. He thought David would not be late again.

He was. Family looked for him in Buick. Cold dinner again, tonight.

October 7. Steven said not to make sandwiches today, he is taking his birthday dollar from Granny to school to buy lunch for himself and David. Susan said how sweet.

Linda, dark braids shining in morning sun, sits on curb, feet in gutter, combing Skipper doll's hair, yelling bye to the boys and Barry, still screaming. They are no longer in sight. I joined her, feet in gutter, to ask why.

Boys promised to draw her a picture in school if she yelled until they could not hear her. "I might be here all day, Mother. You should go on in and do your work."

Susan teased Steven when he asked why she was in bed. "I've been thick," like Linda. She's not amused. "And you know what elth you've been?" Linda asks Susan. "You've been thtupid!"

Red Clay Bank.
Owner requests mothers keep children off steep area on Lena Avenue bank so it will regrow. The children dig roads in it, nothing will grow there.

Today, David and one of accountant's twins set fire to grass on top of the bank. Fire truck terrified us.

Twin hid under his house afraid of police. How Come, the curious twin, cried, "You won't take my brother to jail, will ya?" David is more worried about what Daddy will say than about any silly old jail.

Linda. In bathtub an hour when we check on her tonight. Three naked dolls lying on floor wear spotless wash cloth sarongs. Linda, still dirty-faced. From red clay bank.

David has cast on arm. Fell off clay bank. Thought he whimpered to ward off scolding. Two more hours before Richard got home to drive us to E.R. I know. I'm a mean old giant, like Linda says, and a mean mother like David's shoe says.

Now he has chicken pox.

Susan is voted treasurer 8th grade. Promised to throw her books away, make room for money collected, take only every third milk nickel for herself. Class liked it. Teacher didn't.

Friend Mildred cut Linda's Betty Davis bangs. Linda wants them to grow so the boys will stop calling her Helmet Head.

David lies on stomach, pokes at hole in front sidewalk with loose pebble. "Someday, I'm gonna' get that ol' rock outta' there!" We tell him he will be an old man.

Steven brought new friend home after school to hear his sister scream. Linda, up from nap, not in mood to accommodate. Steven says, "Hold your ears, she can scream louder than anybody!" Linda says, "Hunh uh."

His friend told her to scream that way again. She shakes head no, boys roll on grass laughing.

Steven keeps misplacing his ball to pitch with Barry, Susan. Told him he should find a special place for his special things. Today, found his dirty baseball on my best dishes.

No more sailor hats and dunce caps! After six dreadful months, pills are available to cure ringworm in nine days!

And David finally has soiled cast with all his friends' autographs sawed off his arm. Wants to save it.

Linda has chicken pox, can't stop scratching. Susan bot her a new funny book, gloves to wear at night, made her promise not to scratch.

Richard took Steven, Susan, Barry for hike up behind Baywood Golf. Barry got poison oak. His mother said thanks a bunch.

Typical morning.
Linda is standing at open front door holding 13 year old Susan's lunch. Steven, David, are sitting on kitchen table to see when bus turns corner. Wants hair pinned with barrettes, before she grabs lunch and runs out door.

Physician in neighborhood shopping center offers me a typing job. Puts Richard in a bad mood all morning.

David asks "Are you and Daddy gonna get a dee-force?" Like chubby little boy on Our Gang comedy who looks like David.

We took children and Barry to Sequoia Park Zoo, let them ride the little train. Steven wears Barry's black felt jacket with white leather sleeves. It will show up in next year's pics on David.

Barry screamed going through tunnel, sullen Richard finally laughs.

David put his arm in feeding tube without a peanut, Bill-the-Monkey grabbed him. Linda screamed, for Steven, didn't want Daddy to know. "We knew Steven would figure it out," she said.

1960. Bad Times. David's last chicken pox not over, or he is allergic to something. One blemish left on his bottom.

Should not have given in to Granny for little ones to go to Cedar Creek Thanksgiving week end. She begged. He came home with a rash that started under his arms. Entire body is covered.

Hospital crowded with contagious diseases. Promised doctor to nurse David at home.

Every four hours he is immersed in ice water to reduce fever; he screams, scratches, claws like a kitten, is wrapped in a bed sheet, then plastic. We hold each other, rock, and cry.

David 7, finally well. No more bed wetting or morning baths. He is proud. Maybe it was all the hugging in little Windsor rocker, maybe no more sleep walking, either.

One night I got ready to shower, he went out front door. Chased him around birch tree in my under things, carried him back to bed. He says I made that up.

Foggy Saturday. Susan is in front room, dancing. Linda, playing with Skipper doll. Barry brought over his cub scout book for boys "since your daddy won't let you join the scouts."

They play Sea Hunt like Lloyd Bridges on TV, following walls around the house, scooting beds, climbing over chests. Don't understand that part but don't ask; at least they are quiet under water.

Pepsi bottle air tanks hang on their backs by string, and no talking to them or they will drown.

Game they play longest in which Linda is allowed to participate - she can't swim - is Hide the Rock. Susan says she is too old for such childishness, can't resist yelling warm or cold.

David's favorite game is Touched You Last. Never tires of it when anyone leaves, always wins. Gets everybody excited. Even me.

Another Sunday. Richard, Susan ride 10 miles on bikes.

Occasionally we say blessing, except Richard and Susan. She would but can't remember, he can but won't. Paste samples under table edge at each child's place. Richard thinks they memorize.

He plays Hit Your Hand with Susan sitting to his right, his hand on table, hers on top, removes his fast enough to hit her hand before she moves it. Always wins, though Susan is quick.

Thursday monthly bridge night. Ladies appreciate when I play dummy, for two reasons. Second reason, I always try new desert. The one night dishes are left, the one morning kids get up early to finish the desert.

Last nite, nut tort without flour, recipe from neighbor who cooked for Folger coffee family in S.F. She has interesting stories about chauffeurs, cooks, upstairs maids, and breakfast pasties.

Richard never remembers names but recognizes dogs who chase MG on way to work. At first neighborhood pot luck night, asks, "Is she the black Scotty?" "He's the beagle?"

Fortunately, did not ask about the insurance man whose dog answers to Gottam Britt. Kids wonder how full his swear jar is, the dog runs away often. Hiway patrolman's wife says her husband's beagle is mentally retarded, runs sideways.

Kids like when Daddy gets upset; pays swear jar ahead. They get the nickels.

Linda tied her shoe first time while boys and she watched Animal Kingdom. Was excited. "Look what I did!" Then again. Still no reaction when she lifted her foot and raised her voice.

Her pride runneth over but the boys are more interested in TV. David, stuck his face one inch from hers, "Linda, guess what! No. One. Cares."

The boys lay on stomachs on floor for TV. Linda sits on their back to watch, doesn't care if it is a brother or Barry.

Wish Susan would read more. Says she's too busy with piano lessons, Campfire Girls. Promised each child one year of piano lessons from neighbor. Boys say no thanks.

Steven, 8, shut door to kitchen when answering phone today. Asks if he could go to someone's house to play school, hunt pretty rocks. Someone is a girl.

We are working on a one-horse costume for boys to wear in Plaza Kiddy Parade. They try to stand beside each other. Silly boys, weird horse. Linda wants to take kitty to Kiddy Parade.

David got hooded sweatshirt dirty, hid it in garage, smuggled navy sweater out, put on halfway down the block. Had been watching his secretive behavior. He turned around, I smiled, waved. He grinned, lifted his hand, went on to school.

Steven wants to know how come David got to wear his Sunday sweater. Keeping things fair - bane of my existence.

Bought grey tweed corduroy pants on sale to go with Sunday sweaters. Catholic uniform. Boys want Methodist pants.

Linda starts school soon, making five yoke dresses, same pattern, different materials, she's practicing her name.

Kids sing happy birthday to me, 33. David gave a hug to grow on. Heaven forbid! "Well you can grow smaller, can't cha?" They look for pennies to buy bubble gum for me after school. I am overwhelmed, they are pleased.

Susan, 14, is excited starting high school. Finished neighborhood junior high with friends because of sympathetic principal. District line recently drawn thru our garage. Asked what if she slept in garage?

She gets upset if teased about the right boy, doesn't mind being teased about others.

Made her bed at four today. Went to horse field to get a green apple, climbed tree, stayed there til dinner.

1961. First Day of School for Linda!
Pinned name tag on her dress, asked if she knew why. Sure, she did "So teacher can say hey you with the name tag on!"

Wants to wear new yellow slicker and boots, it is sunny, she doesn't care.

On Susan's first day, took pictures, every one kissing, waving, hugging goodbye. Today we told Linda she better hurry or she would miss the bus.

She went up the hill, one brother on either side gloating, "You won't li-i-ike it, Linda!"

Richard, kids, rode bikes twenty miles. All came home bleary-eyed. Did not know, until pictures were developed, they climbed billboard on freeway to eat potato chips, drink pop. What was Richard thinking! There is surely a law.

Susan baby-sat for Home Economics teacher. Made $6.00.

She cooked a week for Home Ec project, stayed within $30.00 budget for six, making Jello, biscuits, cornbread, picking berries. Every night we had entre, salad, dessert. She cooked, I cleaned.

One day, shopped for economical leg of lamb. Butcher removed bone, we asked for it for Granny. Susan whispered butcher didn't know Granny had dogs. We got church giggles, had to go to another part of store.

Richard hates lamb. Used lots of seasoning, garlic. He didn't know.

Linda and I went shopping today. She wore Betty Boop Halloween lips, dared me to wear them to bank window. I wouldn't. I'm no fun.

Home in time for bakery truck. Neighbors visit in street. Get warm loaf of cinnamon bread, margarine it, for children playing in yard. Thank heaven all 56 children in this double block are not in yard at once.

Thought our subdivision was in the country - mile and half from Plaza - but vegetable truck, milk truck, fish man and even the dry cleaner delivers.

Richard and I discuss girl one year older than Susan who dates older boys. He asked, "Wonder if she is in business?" thinking Susan would not understand. She assured us the girl was in business last year.

Susan and girl friends can dance in garage now. Richard installed speaker to keep racket out of house. Made pizza, sent them there with their music. "Other people have warm family rooms, Daddy."

Richard says turn on the dryer, kill two birds, one stone. She says he will never understand Anything.

Saturday night. Six of us in bathroom. Richard in tub covered with bubble blanket, reading flight magazine, let Linda in to go. Susan used mirror, I needed something out of cupboard. Boys came in just to see if they fit. Linda screams.

Richard: "Now this is a real family room," then shooed us all out.

Linda asked Steven to look at TV with her. He told her to get out of his room, slammed door. Later, wearing Richard's WW11 leather ear flap helmet and flight boots he came out, watched Space Man with her.

Games children play on a cloudy day. Their favorite, My Favorite Secretary staring Ann Southern:

David: I can't pay my rent bill today, Mr. Sands.

Steven: You pay it Friday. Tum te dum. It is Friday, now.

David: I still can't pay!

Steven: I'll give you ten... 1,2,3,4 -

Passing through the room, I tell them landlords do not hit renters.

Steven: Well, they do David!

David: Steven won't do it again, Mother, if we can finish our game. Next time I'll pay-up before I get hit.

Linda, I mean, Katy my favorite secretary, will you show this gentleman where Mr. Sands' office is?

Linda: I'll be glad to. Do you want to follow me, sir? We'll go this way, and around the coffee table here, see, and over this way and don't hit the TV or Daddy'll be mad.

Linda tells them Mother said when she gets ready, - when she gets good and ready - she'll make hot chocolate. It will be their coffee.

David: Thank you, Katy, I'll have a cup with two clumps of sugar.

Linda: You dummy! Hot chocolate already has sugar in it and it's not clumps.

David: Well, you're the dummy. Don't you know how to play office coffee?

Linda: I wish Mother was good and ready, now.

David: Don't bother her. If she's not good and ready, she'll be good and mad and I won't like it and neither will you.

Valentine's Day.
Planned to decorate white cake with Red Hots. David returned with his favorite Kandy Korn.

Under cake, a Home Ec pattern for Susan, pencil sharpener for Steven, funny books for David and Linda.

Today, used ruler I was working with to swat Steven's seat for being rude. He takes the ruler, puts it back on top of the refrigerator by the baskets, laughs and leaves.

Richard, Susan, and I went to church, the rest to Sunday School. Richard promised to go once a year whether he needs it or not but dislikes communion which we always hit on his annual visits.

He and Susan share Butter Scotch rum hard candy, raising noses beyond our pew.

Linda stays home with me afterward. The rest ride ten miles on bikes. David, on Barry's little old, red bike. When anyone went slow on the racers, David rode a circle around them.

A Saturday.
Backed Buick out so Steven could get his bike to get loaf of bread. Susan begged me to take car. Table was set, everyone hungry from yard work, no license and barefoot but Susan said pooh what could happen as all the kids jumped in.

I flood-stalled car at store. Richard brought my shoes, worked on Buick while I drove his stick shift M.G. home with the children complaining they wanted to wait and ride with Daddy. Jerked all the way home in the one gear I knew.

Dinner one hour late. Steven can make it on his bike in eight minutes.

David kissed me good bye for school, face looked spotty. "I got pimples," Pulled up his shirt. There, too.

Took him to bed. He is not going to kiss me ever, anymore, never!

Found him playing in garage. He says washing machine talks, "David's gonna' get in trouble, David's gonna' get in trouble."

He laughs when I carry him back to bed, "I coulda' got away if I tried, just wanted to see how strong you were."

David is now coloring. All the children have spotted faces.

Today, boys took two bananas for lunch, saying lunch is supposed to be a snack. I added a a boiled egg. They had heard us talking about being frugal. Made two peanut butter sandwiches told them they were frugal. Now it is frugal butter.

Tonight Susan asked Steven when it is so cold, rainy, isn't he glad he has a nice warm home. Steven, "Yes, I think about that and sometimes I feel like crying." She called him an idiot stick.

Barry's older sister took the children and Barry to the park so I could nap. David thinks the beauty queen has a neat convertible, "It has mushrooms growing right inside of it."

Linda has measles. I slept with her. Susan took sleeping bag into front room. Linda slept most of today. Kept her busy with kaleidoscope and crayons. Thought her carnation bubble bath would help. Made it worse. Bad Mother.

David. Infatuated with Napoleon hairdo, wets hair, combs it forward to a point. Susan says he looks like a hood. Today he let me re-comb it for class picture. He has such nice light brown hair. He grins.

Linda is invited to skating party. She's excited, friend's sixth birthday, says she will do a ballet on skates, if she can stand up.

Class knows her mother and daddy sleep together, that the kids don't, that she has bread and milk for dinner, was born in an orphanage that had yellow tooth paste.

When she was little, I looped my nylon stocking loosely around her ankle to keep her in crib five minutes. Sat outside door to undo it when she fell asleep. Heaven forbid they should hear her version of that one!

Show and Tell is prize fodder for Teacher's Lounge, I'm certain of it.

Steven still has occasional headaches from his spill. He put reins on bike handlebars, learned they don't work on turns, walked home from clay bank, found me in the kitchen, "What's happening to me, Mother?" slumped at my feet. Never saw anyone faint before.

Steven has application for Little League. Says he could clean elderly neighbor's flower bed to earn fifty cents. Little League costs two dollars, then uniforms, transportation, etc.

House payments have gone up to $92 a mo.

Susan, 15, has survived term without paying class dues. Says its her hard-earned money and since she's not attending school parties, dances or activities, she shouldn't have to pay anybody anything. Richard encourages her.

David hates to mow lawn. Ends up doing his Saturday chore on Sunday. Barry's mom looks across fence, sees him lying on grass moaning. "Poor little David," she says. He repeats, "Yeah, poor little David," so I can hear.

Windy cold day at beach. Susan and girl friend drew circle hopscotch in sand with sticks. Boys play in icy water on an old raft, roasted hot dogs.

Got home, didn't see David's new shoes. Cut old tennis shoe sole to fit into another that had a hole in bottom. He went to school today fussing at stupid shoe, hates talking shoes.

Found his new ones in car, he'll be happy.

Steven came down hall wearing towel draped, tucked at waist, like Daddy. Hair combed, like Daddy.

Barry's sister came over to model strapless formal. Richard asked, "Where's your shirt?" He thinks dancing is primitive but what does he know, him and his two left feet?

Went to church with Susan. She heard a bird, cocked her head listening, wanting to be outside. Counted minutes, turning at intervals to clock to see if she was correct.

Boy in front of us took off his shoe. So did she, couldn't get it back on.

Got giggles getting quarter out of my pocket, dropped it, watched it roll. Liked when he handed it back. When we sang from hymnal she tried reversing every other word.

Now, lying on her stomach on kitchen table, knees bent, white pumps in the air, still in green wool skirt with fringed pockets, white Sunday blouse, reading my Jubilee Trail for book report. Wants me to tell plot so she won't have to finish it.

Today's chores:

- Check David's math papers.
- Cut Linda's bangs.
- Remind Susan no friends on week evenings; put records back in jackets, return my umbrella to its cover, put my rain hood in closet, lipstick in my purse. Someone is getting neck of her blouses soiled, use wash cloth every night.
- Tell Steven about skates on front porch.
- Sew David's pillow.
- Take feathers out of Linda's, too firm and high.
- Bed scrapes wall, move it.
- Plus etc.

Linda. Lost a front tooth, is upset, it was her st tooth, said she had just learned to use it.

Steven tells David about his history lesson, "See, I'm Columbus and you're an Indian and I say, hey, do you mind if I discover America?" David thinks its funny. Steven's teacher didn't.

The boys walk on stilts under Susan's window to spy. She is studying, yells. If she did not, they would stop. Richard says he'll saw them off. They laugh. I don't believe him, either.

Steven. Walks home two miles, from church, so he can stay for Jr. Choir practice. Hope Susan will join adult choir. Everyone needs a place to sing.

Last time I sang around the house, Richard asked if anyone ever told me I could sing. Pleased, I answered no, waiting. He said, "And they won't, either." I don't anymore.

College. Richard is reading Aristotle, drives seven miles home for sandwich then to HSU for English course, then back to work.

When he gets twenty eight teaching units, could teach a trade school or prison. He quit high school for Navy before eleventh grade.

1963. Disneyland.
Withdrew $ from bank for material for Linda's dress, matching shirts for boys. Richard's shirt glowed in dark on ride there on one trip. Do not want children to know we went. Packed his special shirt to surprise them.

Susan, 17, decides to go, night before.

Made arm rests to separate kids in back seat.

David, Steven, Linda swim in public pool in Santa Barbara on the way. David asks Negro boy if he could feel his hair. They trade turns.

Susan said later, she hadn't wanted to visit museums, art galleries, alone. Wanted to go with us. Who can figure seventeen year olds?

And everybody's clothes glowed on tunnel rides!

Family let me desperately steer boat to save our lives while they laughed uproariously. Who told them it was on tracks?

My safety bar would not lock on Matterhorn ride. Richard held it and me, laughing all the while at my terror.

Good to be home. Newspaper reported a woman died falling off Matterhorn ride.

1964. Senior Play. Guys and Dolls.
Susan practices until nine every night at theater. Has walk-on in each act - cigarette girl, Texas wife. Wears white swim suit in one scene.

She just left for friend's house, said she had picked up after herself: Coffee table is full of curlers, brush, hairnet; bathroom has curlers, pajamas, front room has shorts, ironing board. Her bed is messy, clean clothes are on Linda's bed.

Susan interviewed at Trinity Hospital. Now a Candystriper.

For weeks boys ate cereal after school, then salad, now, beans in pie pan like TV cowboys.

Linda unhappy. Boys won't let her be their nurse. Steven said they are not going to get wounded. "We just die for ten minutes, then we are someone else." Linda wants to be their nurse until they are alive again.

This morning. David has just finished oatmeal, is going to ride on motor cycle with paperboy and throw papers, hopes to learn route, get job.

After two weeks, didn't get it.

Almost finished Susan's formal. Spent my Green Stamps on steam iron. Cleaners charge $3.00. Dress was Barry's younger sister's, white nylon, tiny pink flowers. Now, with pink sheet ruffles graduated down back.

Last dance, yellow taffeta matron of honor dress of mine, turned backwards - She doesn't have busts either.

Boys would like to join Boy Scouts but Richard keeps them busy. Took them, Barry, on bike ride "shortcut" to the beach, climbed fence, carried bikes through barn yard muddy manure, pop on Steven's bike exploded going down steep Bella Vista hill on way home. Great ride, they said.

Susan's $26.00 tax refund arrived. She washes dishes at Big Four Italian restaurant where Barry works. He taught her how to cut lobster.

School counselor suggests Susan forego shorthand, typing. He says waitress job can pay for college. What if she doesn't get to college?

Typical Saturday:
8:00 - l0:00
Washed dishes, Linda dried.
Washed cupboards with Purex.
Cleaned chrome chairs and Formica table.
David washed oven. I redid with cleaner.
Changed sheets.
Hand washed nylons.
Sewed button on Richard's pajamas.
Hand-washed kids' red clay socks, bleached.
10:00 - 1:30
Mopped floor, waxed.
Susan got up, had breakfast, left dishes.
David, Linda, folded towels.
Cleaned bathroom.
Had 35 min. coffee next door with Mildred, children cluttered kitchen.
Had Steven sew on button he ripped off David's shirt.

2;00 - 2;30
Made cake.

Put collar snaps on Richard's shirt.
Too busy after 2:30 to keep track.

Easter. Did not dye eggs. Boys spent three days at Granny's. Steven left homemade card for us, glued on two cherry chocolate eggs:
To you:
Things are happy and things are sad
But when your in bed, I'm mighty glad.
Sometimes your mad and sometimes your not
But when your happy you have more jokes
than a comedians got.
From Me. Steven

David, playing in bright sun with neighbor's dog, one hand shading his eyes, the other shading the dog's.

Steven got an F. Asked for help. Wanted to do lesson over even if he got no grade.

David. Keeps my glasses full of flowers, wild ones, tame ones, mine, or neighbors. Still finds water to play in, always wet, muddy.

He's been entertaining family lately at table. Asks for water, milk, shuffles feet, says he'll do it, knowing I will jump up, I'm closer. They've all been getting away with his trick, laughing at me.

Richard had speech in evening Audio Visual class. He worried. Me too, as if he were a child in Christmas pageant. Humourous directions for putting on mechanics coveralls. Lay them on floor, match arms and legs. Class laughed. He is pleased.

Susan made D on report card. She's grounded, thinks it means only dating and we give in to library study, ushering at plays, etc. Life is hard for her. And me.

Boys can hardly wait till Richard takes them on The Hike to Lake City to look for Rattlesnake Dick's gold. They don't go anywhere without their canteens - even to bed.

Law student working at airport is taking marshmallows and steaks. One mechanic, ex soldier, is taking a real machete. The boys' are made of cardboard and duct tape.

After trip David came in front door, "Mom, that was a real man's trip!" fell face down on floor, his back pack still on, slept for two hours. Had 28 large mosquito whelps on his little back.

Richard told about David leaving heavy pack at bottom of steep hill, refusing to carry it up to campsite. Steven put unopened can of beans on fire. Can blew up, put David in good mood, he went down for his pack, climbed back up, still laughing at Steven. No gold.

David. Plays ball tag with boy who is "real neat." Has girls chasing him, twelve years old and smokes. David, impressed.

Today after dinner took walk up the hill. Linda, Steven sneaked through yards instead of going round the block, hid in bushes to scare us, came home same way.

Linda. Waited at window for rain to stop today. She doesn't care, took umbrella out, skated anyway.

Steven is working on tiny signalman for airplane carrier. "See, every movement means something to the pilot so a fly comes buzzing by and the signalman tries to swat it off and the pilot is going nuts making figure eights and all kinds of stuff!"

David thinks that's neat. They embellish till both are laughing. "So, then, the signalman scratches his nose and..."

Trucker's wife took children to skating rink. Steven paid his way, bought dress loafers with shoe shine money. Richard and I rode bikes to watch.

Singin' in the Rain. Everyone did chores early to see TV. David swept everything up in a pile, left it, Steven tended to garbage. Susan, in bed, told Linda, "If I don't see the movie, I don't have to work."

Later, she came to kitchen to hear it on the kitchen speaker, while she fixed her lunch.

Susan placed first in local history speech tournament. We made jumper out of Richard's grey striped Mafia suit, bought pink cotton sweater for San Francisco finals.

He drove. We took Susan's girl friend with. Let them go early on bus by themselves. Susan came in second, won plaque.

Girls had not wanted to go on bus alone. They wanted to be with us. Who knew?

Sewed today. Tapered legs of Steven's and David's hand-me-over pants. David likes skin-tight; Steven does not.

David said at breakfast maybe he wouldn't be doctor, maybe a scientist. Has salamander in muddy bucket, ugly thing, worries me.

Went to concert at university for paper Richard had to write for night class. Took Linda, David, left Steven to answer phone if Susan called for ride from work.

Earlier, found her walking home, late for waitress job, had white skirt uniform with me, - made from Richard's Navy whites. She changed in car.

David wore sun glasses in dark auditorium. Richard said he was about to try them so he could sleep. David threatened to drop glasses from balcony during intermission.

When it was time to leave David was up to his elbows in the fountain. He went headfirst to his waist in freezer today at store, legs in the air.

Hiking, he runs way ahead. Richard says David follows his heart all the way with nothing to back him up, then he poops out. Steven is wary, more careful. Now if we can only get them to share a few of their strengths with each other, he says.

Susan has had bad year, has a plan, won't be home long. Friends, school counselors, Granny, all of us tugging, giving advice. School counselor actively involved in her dating choices, gives her rides.

Friend says we "cannot keep her light under a bushel." Granny offers to keep her mail, etc. safe.

Susan burned Granny's letter, says never mind, "no boy is more important than family."

M.G. in pieces. Again. Embarrassing to put hood up in public, especially now. Newspapers report small foreign cars being pushed over.

Richard rushes home, lays under car, listening to tapes for Music Appreciation exam, forgets name of the guy with the mustache but remembers that German water music man.

Haven't told him dryer won't dry, washer won't wash, agitator is agitated to a nub. He says these days are busiest in his life.

He thinks he's busy. I've been laundromatting for six weeks. Today someone accidentally took my sheet load from dryer.

David likes being in a play. Walked home yesterday at noon for special shirt and Steven's sun glasses - Steven not pleased - for rehearsal.

And again today to get my red muumuu for dentist's red-headed daughter, the one we thought was a boy when she was little because she wore coveralls like David, had a low voice, pixie haircut. Still has.

Richard's back trouble's back again. Boys cut handle, put on rubber tip. They say he walks like a crab, sideways, tease him a mop handle away. He is not amused when pain involved, mainly his.

A Saturday morning. The boys wouldn't let Linda see cartoons, she wasn't dressed. "We had to." She dressed, put pajamas on over, wrapped blanket around, to bug them, she said.

Slumber party for Susan. Made poncho of black material, red scraps, suggested she iron my white slacks. She thought they wouldn't look good. I ironed them. She looked fine.

Today Susan came home teary-eyed; afraid she won't get to go to college. We promised each child $30 tuition at local university - within walking distance - to see how serious they are.

Her friends are going out of town which is her idea of "going to college."

1964. Susan's high school graduation night.
Helped serve Safe and Sober breakfast at 2:00 a.m. Didn't see Susan. Must have missed her.

Presents from family and neighbors, crystal beads, purse, compact, fountain pen. Made white coat and pink sheath. Girl friend gave her an artichoke haircut.

Five kittens climbing drapes and sheers for a week. Linda 9, chooses Chris with bobbed tail. Granny took back four, did not thank her for leaving one.

Steven on patrol, cut full page Vietnam soldier from magazine, copied it combat boots to jacket. Camouflaged toy gun with Richard's masking tape.

Insignia on back of jacket does nothing for his image. It reads Surfin' Honey, last month's interest. Now he says only Momma's boys do that dance. With girls!

Another Fathers Day.
Steven up at 5:00, left note, "Mom, Pop, I had a cup of cocoa and went with Tom to golf course." Caddied 8 hrs. for $1.00. Bought small trophy inscribed Best Dad in the World.

Barry's step dad, Tom, hires Steven, David to shoeshine at his barber shop on Plaza. Boys trade Saturdays. Can't work together.

Teacher decides whose quarter rolled on floor today. Linda, classmate, held on to it. Teacher decided it belonged to other girl, mentioning Linda's father is a mechanic. Linda doesn't understand why Daddy was mentioned since Mother gave her the quarter. She learned two lessons today.

Steven. At end of a cold, did not want to stay in bed. Came to kitchen in long tee shirt, skinny legs like a crane - sun-tanned David calls him mayonnaise legs - said in a high voice, "If you are sick, stay in bed. If you are well, you have to go to work, have to go to work!" Said I was a nag. I hadn't said a word. Do I really sound that shrill?

He went on bike to barbershop without lunch. Sent David with fried egg sandwich.

Boys would not touch a cold egg before, especially Steven, but that's what Tom takes. Had to learn to break the yellow at the right second to spread over white, then cool.

Mildred sent Barry to our house to learn to eat frugal-butter sandwiches.

Steven showed me some model airplanes, did not want David to know. Later, he offered David one. Said it is no fun flying alone.

To read some quiet Monday in the future:

- After coping with Richard, Susan and friend, Steven and friend, Linda and friend, David and friends, all weekend, I intended to go back to bed.
- Almost went to sleep.
- Granny, Grandpa came for weekly lunch. Made tuna sand., deviled eggs. Cleaned up.
- Susan returned from classes, turned on TV, cluttered kitchen.
- Two girl friends came at 2:00, cluttered kitchen. All those glasses are mine?
- David and Steven came at 4:00 for snack, more clutter.
- Richard at 6:00.
- Susan home at 7:00 before library job. More dishes. Needs a ride home at ll:00.

1965. Another Valentine Day.
David, 12, went to store, then directly to bedroom before bringing groceries to kitchen.

Lifted his wrinkled pillow, found a valentine "To a Dear Girl." At dinner, asked who he would give a valentine to this year. If he gave one. He said, "Oh, maybe Teach." I smiled.
"Well, I was going to have Daddy change Dear Girl to Dear Teacher." Richard laughed.
Later he asked Daddy to write From David real nice.
Richard offered to scratch out Dear Girl and substitute Teacher.
David tore up the valentine.

Richard has stare-downs with the children. Linda to Steven, "Let's have a stare-down with my leather skunk." He gave it for her 10th birthday. "He won't blink for 20 years."

Tried to teach Linda to play with her birthday jacks. Enjoyed it more than she did. Played alone.

Last year Steven fussed over his hair, getting wavy. This year, is meticulous about clothes, spends more time mussing his hair.

Susan: "Guess who's getting handsome?" Now he won't even carry a comb.

David says he will drive a log truck when he is 18.

Steven: "Me, too. Teach school in winter and drive truck in summer." Like his teacher.

Susan registers at Humboldt State.
Richard gave her $30 fee. She earned $600 last year. Finds that is not enough. She left $5 many times to help with groceries.

R. Gives speech in Audio Visual night class, about wife eating crackers in bed, class laughs. He likes captured audience.

Steven's class is having party and graduation dance, 8th grade. He's not interested, but David is.

Family watched Lonely are the Brave with Kirk Douglas on TV. Steven wants to write a great story like that.

Steven: Welp, I'm finishing my sixth year at the barber shop and I don't care how much I have to pay for a haircut from now on! Boy, that was an education!

David: Did you ever get those guys who say, 'Now, son, if you just take a nylon stocking...' That's like Pops sitting there eating, telling Mom how to cook a good meal.

Steven: In the Varsity once while I was havin' ice cream this Old Man was talkin' real loud.

David: How old was he?

Steven: He was old, had to be pushin' thirty. So he sends me for cigarettes. He was crackin' jokes like, What's a cookie? It's a virgin doughnut. The nice lady who sings in the church choir and owns the shop made a face at him.

David: Yeah?

Steven: Yeah. Man, he's sure been around. He won $1700 at cards over in Eureka, but was busted broke. He had $2.00 on him. The one with the big head, little shoulders, a scarf with a bobby pin in it, and cowboy boots. One man, 65, had been in jail, was celebrating being out - and got in again. When he came into the shop, he asked me to take him to the bathroom.

David: Then, what did you do?

Steven: I did, and started to go back out front when he said for me not to go and man was I nervous. I helped him 'cause he was drunk and kept my hand behind me on the door knob and he reached for me right while he was standin' there goin'.

David: Did you ever get the one with the toupe, T-bird, wrap-around sun glasses - you know, that wears white shoes?

Steven: Oh yeah, him.

David: And I didn't know what color to use.

Steven: Neutral.

David: Yeah, that's what I did and he asked if I use white. I told him no. Neutral and shine. So he asked what if the color was worn off. I told him but its not.

Steven: Yeah, men don't wear imitation white, anyway. They wear leather.

If no one claims the jacket left in barber shop, in three weeks David gets it. Steven hid it for him.
Sees the disapproval on my face.

Steven: Okay. Okay. I'll put it back in Lost and Found!

Protein diet. Susan lost seven pounds. I haven't. At a pound a year, what will I weigh on fiftieth anniversary? If I live that long. We were hungry for fruit, ate a whole can of peaches.

Ma and Pa.
Neighbor brought potful of candle fish. Boys offered to help clean them, eager to use their knives. Hid them after they carved neighbor's fence. How did they find them?

Linda gingerly carried one to her room to meet her goldfish.

Steven finished cutting heads, started toward David, dripping fish entrails, yelling "I'm Frankenstein, hate live, love dead!"

David, "Let me kill 'em, Ma, let me kill 'em, Pa!" Took their knives away again.

We have suddenly become Ma and Pa. Susan called Richard Daddy in art class, raised eyebrows. Okay, just so it isn't Maw and Paw.

This afternoon.
David burning trash in fireplace, wearing paper hat, nylon stocking like a bandit, from wastebasket.

When Pa came home, David asked, "Well, what have you got to say for yourself, Pa?" He is learning to get around Pa's moods, copying his gruffness. David looked so ridiculous, Pa had to laugh.

Steven. Stubbed his toe, Pa told him to write his own excuse. Wants me to sign it.

School has collection of foolish notes on which Pa collaborated. Some with a different color crayon used for each word. Trucker's wife is school secretary.

After school Steven works in neighborhood grocery store, says that's exercise enough. He and Pa think riding the sillybus then taking P. E. is more than stupid.

David asked his friend to hold the phone while he called me to window to see birds on the clothesline. I laugh. "Oh, Ma. They're not doin' that." Asked me not to tell anyone, forgetting his friend could hear and would tease.

Steven told David to ask Susan about the ducks she saw on the way to San Francisco when we attended Speech tournament. She chased one away from another. David laughed, "Life sure is stupid, isn't it?"

I asked Pa if he talked with the boys. Grinning, says sure he does, all the time. Said he learned everything in Navy and they can, too.

Next time they got close to the subject, I make sure they know girls are treated like ladies, not dogs. They now identify certain individuals as woman doggers.

Steven slept in his "crow's nest" for a while, a square shelf Pa built high in far corner of garage. Terrific wind "tornado" deposited flying piece of neighbor's plywood on roof over his head, terrible noise, we need new roof.

He moved to bunk shelf Pa built in bike shack. Too many colds, he's back in room with David.

My birthday. Boys got helium balloon, sang falsetto, like Alvin and Chipmunks. Hope they don't get sick.

Took two weeks to get hair in page boy. Asked Pa if he liked it. "Sure," he says, "Always have."

Not affectionately demonstrative. Occasionally I ask if he loves me just to hear children laugh at his usual red-faced answer. "I live here, don't I?"

Mildred brings Lady Chatterly's Lover over in brown paper sack. Saw it in Barry's room, wants to get rid of it. "The man puts flowers in Lady C.'s hair!" she says. I say, "So?" Oh.

She leaves it for me. I read, rip, burn, read, rip, burn. Wonder if it was library book?

Will we ever get our $9,000 house loan paid off and how much interest in thirty years? If we live that long.

Susan wants to move out. Says Linda can come live with her. I cringe. Granny has offered tiny cabin in town where she and Grandpa retreat from Cedar Creek snows.

1967. August 9. Susan's birthday, 21. Asked if she would like something she's never had. She's thinking champagne, I'm thinking bagel. Pa got a blue sweat shirt for her.

Steven. Another Erickson at Hartsooks. Susan worked at the river resort as housekeeper last summer. Good to separate boys for the summer.

It always starts out serious, "Stay on your side of the room! That's not your drawer!" Always ends up a laughing, wrestling game. Was not always that way. Steven's baby-biting quickly escalated to body clashes until David was about eleven.

Steven came to the kitchen holding his nose sounding more proud than hurt, "You know, that David socked me in the face. He's got a real wallop!"

Steven has been home three times this summer. Still growing. "Ma, Hey! They remodeled the store, lowered all the counters. I can even see the girls walking in the next isle. Didn't use to be able to reach the chocolate cupcakes!"

Today he planned to do something I didn't approve of. Sitting on the floor, barefoot, cutting out a pattern, I looked up, shook my finger, told him he was not going to do it. He asked why. "Because I'm the mother!"

Looked down his 6' 2" at me, laughed. "I know," he said as he left, "Isn't it awful?"

David brought five marbles to me in bed this morning. "They're yours, now don't lose them." Doesn't think I get it. Left with his books to get homework done between shoe shines.

Was seen two miles away with older boy, smoking. "Oh, Ma! I just did it to show off." Grounded.

Susan. Serious about roommate of ex-boy friend. Have not met him, away at college in bay area on scholarship.

She hasn't decided to marry where he attends school or here in Arcata. Says maybe she doesn't need a wedding dress.

Bought $10 worth of embroidered cotton, Fransay, white on white, and $5.00 taffeta lining, on sale.
Basic dress made. Slim, fitted, with boatneck. Enough material to make straight back panel. Taffeta pantaloons for surprise under modern dress. She likes it.

His Mother called, wonders how to suggest her son get his hair cut, asked how Susan will wear her hair, doesn't want them to have hippie-look.

Paul cut off goatee. Susan trimmed his hair. Hers is full, straight to ears with side part.

Susan sat in middle of our bed, made veil in one hour with bits, pieces of satin-covered wire from a bridesmaid bouquet, formed a crown. Has been bridesmaid three times. Linda will wear pink dotted Swiss bridesmaid dress of Susan's. She's 13.

Day before wedding 5:00 p.m. Nervous about rehearsal tonight. Pa won't go without a fuss, but maybe with Mother here... I'm seeing spots.

Steven told Pa he had to go, made me lie down to avoid migraine, then sat on floor like door stop to keep everyone out, long legs stretching across hall.

Pa found he knew Paul's father from one winter job at plywood mill. Didn't help my migraine. Still had all the aura.

Saturday. Mother and I picked bridal bouquet from yard - silver sage, ivy, pink Cecil Bruner buds, Pa's bachelor buttons. Pretty.

1967. December, 17.
Susan, still in bed, tells us to quit talking about wedding. "I don't want to think about it!" Sun out, then turned cloudy, windy, rained on way to church. Put on her short veil, snapped panel train on shoulders in vestibule. All brides are beautiful. Paul agrees.

Granny drove 60 miles round trip through terrible weather leaving Grandpa at snowy Cedar Creek to take care of mill, dogs, cats, road so she could get back in.

Pa missed Susan's cheek, kissed nose, ceremony over in 20 minutes.

Wedding of the Season:
Policeman's son marries mechanic's daughter in $60.00 wedding, two families in attendance, at groom's church. Susan doesn't want picture in paper.

Next day. David tells Steven something stuck in his throat, a sort of bumpy thing, while Susan was up there in church.

Steven: Yeah, I had that too. Couldn't swallow and it hurt.
David: It was when the minister said Susan Erickson.
Steven. I kept thinking, that's my sister up there.

Susan left a little note on blue art paper:
"Nothing written on paper will express every emotion felt for a family - suppers of beans, dinners of turkey, blessings written under our plate, and years and years of laughing with lots of funny faces.
I will be living with Paul but always carrying my first family in my mind. Just thank you for these memories and being alive."

Saturday Night Special.
For years, Susan's favorite was pizza and Seven-Up. We asked Steven what his will be.

Hamburgers, he quickly answers. Did he want French fries with that? "Naturally!" I hate making those things. For here or to go? Oh, Ma.

Steven already sitting at end of table where Susan last sat. David is in Steven's old chair anticipating Pa's hit-your-hand game.

I keep looking for Susan. She has never left the house without me watching her go. She never knew.

First child gone. Have to get acquainted with the other children.

1967. End of December.
Pa Laid Off after 11 years! Economy bad. Financial Consultant's report stated two employees had to go. Tension all around.

Pa made second landing at emergency field on Kneeland to gage troublesome tree approach. Ten minutes late back to airport. First to get pink slip.

He's packed for San Francisco, United Airlines. Never saw him so down, so unsure.

1968. Friday, 13 Feb. I'm hired at HSU!
After 21 years at home supervising four children, two collies, four cats, four birds, one rat, one mouse, two goldfish, could have been chained to dusty book cart in the musty bowels of the Library, slated to be imploded, and never seen again.

Chose thirteenth typing desk in business office. Scary, but more pay, $405 mo! Rumor: "Assistant Business Manager hired an older woman this time." I am 39.

Personnel Director dictated letter at 80 wpm. Not one word from Susan's records! Used Chances Are and Moon River for shorthand practice.

Arrived home to kitchen full of laughter. Pa brags chicken hash wine, gravy hash wine, even the potatoes and cole shlaw. Didn't know he could cook.

I cook every day after dinner for next day. Tonight, bean soup, ravioli casserole, custard pie for tomorrow.

Today came home to breakfast dishes in sink, messy house, table not set. Put all food away except frugal butter, jelly, bread. Slammed nine white cupboard doors shut.

Everyone stayed away from me in bedroom. Someone cleaned kitchen, David fried chicken for tomorrow night's supper. Kids made themselves sandwich. No punishment there, they like PBJs. So do I. Pa, not so much.

Linda has cough, home today, Barry's mom checks on her. Barry stayed with us after school when Mildred had to work. He and Steven snickered over naked natives in National Geographic.

Linda embroiders, takes care of cat, starts supper, peels potatoes, sets table.

Three mo. later.
Pa gets part-time job at other flying service at airport. The other pink-slipper, ditto. Bank account down to $400.

I like working. First Performance Report rated my skills a bit rusty. Just because I didn't know what File 13 was or coded a Purchase Order for a pallet of ivory folders?

One of first typing duties. Created circular for auction of older houses to be removed from campus. First one moved down the hill to Arlington Way. Beginning of upgrade for that little neighborhood.
Type checks. Today one reads Pay to Susan Erickson, $50, book money. She waits on hall floor for student loan with rest of hippies. Her work study job will repay.

1968. Pa Registers Full Time at HSU!
Took all summer deciding to attend full time. After bills paid, wanted to buy a nice present for him before quitting work. He jokingly said he couldn't think of anything better than being able to study.

This, from the boy who quit school before 11th grade to join Navy, the man who hates to read directions and who has only read one book. Tom Sawyer. Dared him to quit part-time work, go to school full time, teach. Even if it is an industrial school or prison.

He balked. Friend-Mildred asked what he would be doing in four years. "I will be 52 in four years!" She asked how old would he be in four years if he did not get a degree.

Pa takes odd jobs. Converts a garage door on next block to picture window. Asked when he learned that. "Today," he says. Tom-the-barber gave him work digging out sewer at Tom's rental. Also received $ anonymously, must have been accountant, it was wrapped in office copy tissue.

Every morning Pa reads note on mirror. "Did you like digging out sewers, fixing city hall roof when noon siren blasts your ear? Where will you be in four years without a degree? A better place?"

Steven worked with Pa on sewer job, didn't like it, either.

This afternoon, Steven found me in supermarket. "Ma, of all places, I'd least expect to see you in funny books." Asked me to buy chili soup for lunch in exchange for picking out comic for Pa.

Kids read them. Any remark from me is met with Pa's lecture that they are true to life, are lessons in psychology. Linda's favorites: Archie, Betty, Veronica. Pa's: Tom and Jerry, Mad, Donald Duck.

Steven waits beside Buick on his green 350 Honda to escort me home. Looks like a highway patrolman. Black helmet, leather jacket. We suggest he might be one like neighbor Bob he admires. "Naw, I could never give anyone a ticket."

Paul graduated. He and Susan rented log cabin here while she finishes her degree at HSU. Paul works in mill until position opens up at HSU.

David worked on ranch, top of Liscomb hill, boarded there, now works at gas station here in town.

Steven found his old baseball mitt. "Got my name on it with a cato pen, in third grade. I was in a hurry to go to recess, but Miz. Graham said I had to wait till she finished printing it for me." Socks his fist in open palm, remembering.

Tonight. David and Steven brought in a blinking saw horse covering a crater the city dug. "Come enjoy it in the dark, Ma!"

This huge red light is flashing Danger! in the front room and they don't understand why anyone should be upset. Frantically chased them out with it, both yelling, Oh Ma!

Steven's Accident:
We're upset long after the danger is over. He slid his Honda into neighbor's parked logging truck.

At 17, Steven's only thought in E. R., "Pa's gonna' be mad at me, isn't he?"

Essay about communication Pa wrote about Steven for class:
"There are times when communication is not manifested verbally. Actions in those instances are sufficient. For instance, on Good Friday my wife rushed home from work in order to change and attend services. Being short of time, she attended the nearest church, around the corner. She had to step over our eldest son's motor cycle torn apart in the driveway.

Halfway through the service someone slipped into the pew to share the book she held. It was Steven with grease under his fingernails, wearing the first white shirt and hastily-tied skinny tie in years.

I know exactly what he was saying by his action: "You don't approve of my motor cycle, it clutters your nice front yard, yet you allow me time to work on it there. You don't really want me to have it. You worry, still you trust me. I appreciate it. Coming to a strange church, any church, in this too-tight shirt on a beautiful sunny afternoon means I will make just as much effort for the family. Thank you."

Steven deserved the A on Pa's paper.

Later, Pa's essay about David:
Sharing an Experience Opens Communication:
Two hours to spend in a strange town with a fifteen year old who cannot make small talk with adults; he likes to be on the move.
So I said we should sit down and figure out where to go. We sat on a bus stop bench at a four-way intersection without stop lights, in a busy city, where we could watch people and things go by. One of my favorite but seldom enjoyed pastimes. We hear clashing gears and smell acrid diesel.

He says, "Man, I bet I could drive one of those."

"Hard on the kidneys," I tell him.

"Is that why he's so fat, Pa?"

"No. The only exercise he gets is between the truck and the diner."

A girl on a Honda goes through the intersection without stopping.

"Hey, Pa, did you see that dumb dame?"

"No, I was watching the old lady in the Mustang peel rubber."

"What old lady?"

"She's gone now."

"Man, I like that rubber smell, it smells good!"

"Ugh! Want to go get a gedunk?"

"Naw! Let's watch a wreck! One's coming up any minute."

"What if they head for this bench?"

"Well, Pa, we'll just jump up on it real quick."

"O.K.! But we better go - our Jeep must be ready - been over two hours."

"So soon? We just got here! Man, I never knew just watchin' people could be fun. I've heard you say how interesting people are but I didn't believe you. Just thought grown ups were just too old to get with the action. Listen, next time we come let's bring Steven. Wait til I tell him about the station wagon with the St. Bernard and the old lady with the cat in the baby buggy. Man I just couldn't watch everyone at once.

1968. May 19. Twenty-third anniversary.
Linda bought chocolate cake, coconut, cherry icing, immediately took it to kitchen, sampled it, all the while humming Happy Birthday.

Grandpa and Pa open kitchen wall.
All three children burned with creosote helping build back deck.

Saturday. Steven, David, looking at cartoons sprawled on front room floor like kindergartners, waiting for Pa to finish coffee. Deck work again today, will save 28 steps instead of going thru garage.

David's parakeet died. "Steven, let's get outa' here." For once Steven was up on time, took cage into garage so David wouldn't see it after school.

David takes Chris-cat to his room every chance he gets. Steven doesn't like it but doesn't throw it out. Linda says its okay for David to borrow her cat for a while.

1970. Saturday Night.
Took Linda and friends to movie Gone With the Wind. First night driving, in rain, fog, seven miles to Eureka. Linda makes jokes about my driving. "Ma runs red lights, stops at green." They were satisfied not to sit with me. Teenagers!

David and Pa went up mountain to dig Granny, Grandpa out of snow. Moon went behind cloud. David, "That's when werewolves come out, Pa." Floundering in three feet of snow, Pa kept saying, "Let's rest, Let's rest." David likes it.

Returned at ll:00 p.m. David still got up in time for school. Steven wouldn't have.

This morning. Up early, made cocoa, French toast. Children usually make their own. David leaned close. I sniffed, smiled. His interpretation of me, "My, don't we smell nice today?"

Sees my bare feet, gets fuzzy slippers, puts them on me. When I cook and spill flour on them, he calls them Biscuit Shoes.

When he was younger he had to wear Susan's hand-me-over white, round-toed, T-strap shoes with cut-outs, those he first called Biscuit Shoes.

Typical evening. Cooked tomorrow's roast beef, potato pancakes.

David, washing dishes, didn't agree with something I said, pulled middle finger of rubber glove out as far as it would go. Pretend I don't see.

Tonight, suggest Steven might bring home something from his job at market, occasionally. Maybe a pie or ice cream on sale? He's shocked, says it is embarrassing I would mention such a thing, is going to talk it over with friend.

David wants to know how come he still has grass stains on his football uniform, no one else has. How come his football team wears white satin knickers? Oh, Ma!

How come I have to know where everything is? Where is work handkerchief? Where is my mitt, my report, my book, a needle, the thread?

Today, served dinner, cooked another one. Asked family for nap time. Within next half hour:

- Linda came in, said no one would help with play she's writing, slammed my door.
- David put Pa's heat vibrator on my back, feet, tried to vibrate the bed.
- Steven stormed in, friend thought it wrong asking him to contribute food from his job.
- Pa came in asking how to spell medicine for paper he writing.

Several nights later. Steven brought giant bunch of bananas store was going to discard, too ripe. We had banana bread. "Maybe I'll bring ice cream next time," he said.

Linda stayed all night with friend, met two boys. Later the older one came to window to get her friend. I called the mother, today. Linda is not going to speak to me again, EVER.

Two hours later she asks me to roll her hair. Love doing it.

Today I asked what Steven believes in:

- I hate titles, ideas that won't settle down.
- Girls who are not Frank. It's a joke, get it Ma?
- I like hushness in libraries.
- Zolo (biker) friends.
- Wind in my face.
- Things by writers even if its not literature for the ages.
- I'm grateful for any thought another soul puts on paper for me.
- The smell of coffee. Why can't it taste like that?

David's list:

- I hate hurts, cavities, conceited people, bad breath.
- I love attention, Me, but I still hate conceited people.
- I like prune juice to lax myselfative. I made that up.
- Things in my pocket to add to my collection.
- Mac and cheese in a bowl with a spoon.
- I believe I could eat a whole ice cream pie by myself.

Weekend. Pa bought a whole ice cream pie just for David. He couldn't eat it.

Boys and Linda went up to Cedar Creek in Jeep with us. They are usually busy, with girl, boy stuff.

Steven showed David how sea gulls court, bobbing his head, squatting his tall frame on narrow top of back seat. David did too, facing Steven, is shorter, head doesn't bump. Balanced on seats, arms outstretched. Their laughter infectious.

Linda told Pa to knock them off. We turned onto Cedar Creek Mill road, he watched mirror, swerved Jeep, put them off balance.

Time running out for Sunday rides. Time was, I couldn't let white baby shoes touch the Buick seat. Or their little hands wear paint off the Fridge.

They showed us a well-worn path out to the big rock high above Hiway 299 on county road to Cedar Creek where they learned to smoke. "But we don't now." They meant, not in front of me.

Their Smothers Brothers' imitation.
Steven, "You know Ma always liked you best," and David, "Well, did you know there's pumas in the crevices in these woods?" Silliness did not stop til we reached Granny's little red house by the old mill.

1970. After High School Graduation.
Steven, quit store job this month, fixing his bike for The Trip to Canada. School paper printed pic on bike for his big adventure before joining Coast Guard.

He asked if he ever told me about:

- The little girl left in parking lot who stopped crying when he put her in basket, took her in the store, told her to stick close to him. She did not say a word, handed him items while he stocked shelves.
- The time he rode his bicycle between isles to storeroom.
- The time he walked into the glass door.

- When he ran into stack of bottles with a line of shopping carts. "It was awful. First six carts kept going and going, slow motion."
- Or about handouts to hippies.

David is standing on the seven-inch window sill to see if he still can.

1970. Second Chick Leaves Nest!
Steven in Coast Guard. Typically, Steven is ready two days early, insists Pa leave for airport hours ahead of time.

Cried first week he left, at work, home, every time I thot about him.

He called from phone booth in New York, yelling above street noise, "Hey Ma, guess where I am!"

He always took two hours making his lunch, frying bacon, onions, opening beans, adding catsup, telling everyone to stay out of kitchen so he wouldn't be late for work at the market. Funny then, so why cry now.

Musical Chairs:
David's Saturday night favorite is fried rice. Got take-out until I learned to make it. Have to cook rice day before.

He is already in Steven's chair by the door. Linda sits beside Pa, is sure she can beat him at the hit-my-hand game.

Steven writes long letters about how the guys had to find a nickel in mud as punishment for talking after lights out, how early he has to be up, what the food is like.

When he was home, he had habit of coming in to ask if everything was alright in the house. No fusses or anything? Said he couldn't be outside unless everything was alright inside.

When he is home he pulls me to daveno for long talks, is proud Pa is in college. He may go when he's out of the Guard. "If they pay."

Sunday. Linda came in bedroom, - family says I live there - announced she had been in every house on this long block. Is that the thought for the day? "Yes, every kid on the block should have been in every house by the time they grow up!" Is she grown up? She takes the red lollipop out of her mouth, "Sure!"

At one time or another every child on this double block was in this house. Developer has six children, named streets for family. We live on his wife's street, they live on his.

One of their little girls used to, without knocking, head for a popsicle in our Fridge. She knew all the houses, streets, and popsicles belonged to her father.

Sunday. This morning Linda rolled tea cart to the bedroom with waffles, bacon, eggs, coffee, violets from front yard. Pa hates eating in bed but we stay under covers for a couple reasons. Handsome breakfast.

Prom night.
Linda is wearing yellow dotted Swiss dress with white collar and cuffs to Friday dance. Date, David's friend, shows up wearing tennis shoes, black tuxedo printed on tee shirt. She wears her tennies, too.

By default, they win King and Queen, girl with most votes absent due to illness. Saturday, wherever Linda goes on her Honda scooter, so goes the crown.

Monday she is called to principal's office. Girl-with-most-votes, mother in tow, cries, presses Linda to relinquish crown.

She's heard its been worn in gym class, all over town. Says Linda shows no respect for the honor. Linda doesn't care, it's hers.

Senior play.
David is in Brigadoon. Wants his kilt mini length. "Won't you be cold?"
Oh, Ma.

Pa comments about my bubble hair and short dress. Flattened my hair, put on calf-length dowdy black knit. Everyone laughs. Linda says it looks like Shagundela. Pa said that was better.

David told his friends, "Bet my Pa is fussing about coming right about now. He always does that."

1971. David, 18, has physical this week.
Anxious about broken ear drum when he was little. If ok, he leaves for Coast Guard.

Pa wants David to go to Cedar Creek, work with him on old highway bridge before he leaves. David wants to go to races in Redding; has 15 cents in his pocket.

Steven's last chore was painting backyard fence he helped build. Pa never did find out which kid in neighborhood used a post hole for a toilet. Swear jar involved.

Grandpa, Pa, David, worked on old county bridge at Cedar Creek. It will last many years after he is out of Coast Guard.

Linda is on Edith Ann kick. Talks through her nose like Lily Tomlin. Incessantly.

Another Easter. Glad that's over. Never did like egg dye on everything. Bad Momma.

Today David and I talked for a long time. He would give all he cares about to have gone on bike trip to Canada with Steven but his bike was lightweight, no money, and Steven, "mostly, hadn't begged." He said Steven was always the leader.

Steven has said he always was envious of David's ability to have fun. "Even rocks and sticks David found were better." Steven laughed at everything David said or did," and David always had lots of friends." Steven, one at a time.

When Steven was first home on leave, David played busy, took no time to talk to him. Second day, David yelled from deck to Steven in yard with Pa, "Don't you touch anything on my side of the room while I'm gone!" Steven rolled on grass laughing.

Sunday. David, typically not ready for 6:05 a.m. departure tomorrow. Still worried about his car parked out front. It leaks when it rains or even frosts. Girl friend will store it.

1972. Third Chick Leaves Nest!
David looked so young in a.m. half-light, hair mussed, too-big boxers, little-boy sleepy-eyed. He dressed in ragged jacket, old cords, like he dressed for work at service station.

At airport, he acts cool, cuts up, sticks his cheek out for us to kiss. Cheek still so soft.

Left to wait in car. Family watched him go out gate to plane, one we used to watch on Sunday rides.

"No more fun, boys all gone," Pa says on way home.

Linda: "You still have me!" He asks what her Saturday night special will be and would she move to the foot of table by the door?

"No way!" she answers. "Whoever sits there has to go out the French doors and I'm not leaving. But we could have fried chicken and potato salad," always her favorite birthday menu.

For two nights, Pa has asked, "What do you suppose David is doing now?"

"You know who you are really going to miss? That busy, noisy, rambunctious -"

"Linda is not going! You can let three go, but you just have to put your foot down sometime."

David writes short notes signed with a smiley face, or only a post-it note "Doin' Stuff!" Does not take the time to write long letters like his brother, was humiliated when girl friend's gift of small Teddy bear was confiscated in presence of bunk mates, shocked at trays of pork chops thrown overboard.

Today, Linda and Pa picked me up at work for pizza at noon. She jumped out of jeep onto fire hydrant, bowed to passersby, patchwork jacket, faded jeans, braids. I hide, Pa encourages her.

He has summer off, has taken her to Weaverville two times for ice cream. Sixty miles on David's motorcycle, out of fog. She talked him into picking berries with her for tonight's pie.

David home on leave. Borrowed $200 from Linda to work on an old truck up on sidewalk, oil and grease everywhere, can't get oil pan on. He bought girl friend $340 sewing machine, now is broke.

Girl friend bought him a drum set last year, neighbors not appreciative.

Will be home a week, doesn't know where he is going. Worried, car not sold yet.

I grudgingly went to church with Linda, wanted to sleep in. She wore my beige Lass O'Scotland knit, baby dress from Granny 17 years ago, now cut in two and skirt lined, which shortened it.

Posed by Buick, making fun of my picture wearing the dress when it was new. Knit was way below my knees, is now way above hers, she looks like her Skipper doll.

I wore new Pendleton suit. Linda, annoyed there was another like it in church.

Couldn't find my place for reading. "I know," she stage whispers, "When they baptize you they give you the secret and we've never been baptized." She mumbled, hummed, began every line in hymnal a note late enough to catch the tune.

Minister suggests those who so desire could approach alter. "So long, Ma, you need it."

Leaving, she tells woman wearing my suit that the woman has excellent taste.

Senior Play: Linda is reporter in senior play Damn Yankees.

Wore my Pendleton one scene. She thought it antique-looking enough.

1973. Linda Graduates.
Chose Chief for name on diploma, Pa's nickname for her. With all the Indian publicity, people surely thought she had some noble cause, even wore braids.

Boy nearby, "Leave it to Linda Erickson!"

She still works at Kentucky Fried Chicken, no carrier on Honda scooter, brings huge bucket home under sweatshirt. Looks pg.

Linda's new job.
Works for engineer on Plaza who drives older white Thunderbird with round side windows. Told him she had driver's license, could type.

Today, in company's huge pickup, she parked, bumped off curb outside my office. Delivers technical land descriptions to university. Didn't know she could type. That well. Or drive. At all! Said David taught her.

Linda Hospitalized.
Completely severed leg ligament in gym class at HSU. Got herself 700 mi. to L.A. for second surgery, home again in cast, on crutches.

Made one coral, one chocolate raw silk slack suit while she was gone. She thought I wanted to hide her 16" scar. Looks like a model.

Last Chick Leaves Nest!
Linda and girl friend move to apartment, giggle, take birds, goldfish. Burned Zonker, Animal Cracker boxes, tore tiger mascot off wall, Pa's bespoke Pink Panther from door.

Left 76 sign, bicycle license plate, coffee can of crayons on window sill. Her yellow walls may stay but orange drapes can finally come down. Took sofa/bed she bought, she and I upholstered.

Yet O heart, nor years, nor sadness
Can destroy our childhood roses.
Where sweet faith abides in gladness,
Faith whose light is immortal day,
Faith whose joy keeps souls in endless May

Mozart

THE END

# The Rest of the Story

1974. While Pa took down orange drapes, I listed a few long-festering complaints:

- I do not like thermostat set at 79. Wear the sweater I knitted for you.
- I have never liked oysters, please stop telling me to taste them.
- Just because you do not like parsley is no reason to put it on my plate.
- Funny papers are not funny to me or I would read them.
- I do not need to be told how and where to park every time I shop.
- Old English movies will not alter my character, no need to change my channel.
- Do not whistle for me, come find me.
- And why on earth did you persist with the Alah-bowing game when the children outgrew it.

He hung on the ladder, eyes wide, mouth open. "IguessIthoughtitwasamildformofpunishmentwhatbroughtthatonatthistimedon'tholdbackistheremore?"

From now on he could do breakfast, I will do dinner, and lunch is up for grabs. But that will do for today.

1975. Pa Graduates at 52. Bachelors Degree, Teaching Certificate.

After maintenance job in pot shop then volunteering in Wood Shop, he now teaches there part time. We don't have to move! He likes lecturing. No surprise there.

1976. Pa completes Masters degree. Wins history award which cash amount he donates to Industrial Arts student loan fund. Cedar Creek Lumber Mill is thesis subject.

1982. New department head consolidates part-time positions to one full time, hires a young doctorate. Pa is laid off.

Pa's mentor Writes Letter of Reference:

"To Whom It May concern,
It is a distinct pleasure to write on behalf of Richard Erickson whom I have known for fifteen years as both a student and later as a valued colleague.

As a student, Mr. Erickson was considerably older than the average but he displayed an eagerness that endeared him to the faculty and his classmates. Because of his abiding interest and background in art I could count on him for clever and pleasing design solutions. He paid meticulous attention to the detail work involved in his wood-working projects. The object he chose to develop in my mass production class has stood as the benchmark for those who follow him.

Mr. Erickson was the obvious choice for a part-time position to handle the multiple sections of Beginning Woodwork as well as the evening classes. He has the most delightful manner of communicating with students of anyone I know. He has the unique ability to keep his students loose while involving them in a classroom atmosphere where learning takes place naturally.

Richard is technically skilled in all phases of woodworking. He has both an understanding and an appreciation of the safe and efficient use and care of tools and machines. I am confident that he can handle woodworking at any level.

In addition to his teaching he assumed the responsibility for the departmental bulletin board. He has made it one of the showplaces of the campus because he catches the humor and significance of the written word, pictures, and cartoons in such a delightful way. His masters thesis was exceptional for a person in our field. It was awarded first prize the year it was written by the Humboldt Historical Society.

Mr. Erickson was a charter member of Epsilon Pi Tau, our national fraternity for outstanding industrial educators.

Any school fortunate enough to secure the services of this gentleman will be assured of a resourceful and highly competent teacher. He can be counted on to take an active part in the affairs of the entire school and the community, as well. I am pleased to say "I hired him!"

Arthur C. Stegeman, Ed. D.
Humboldt State University"

Children, cars, and house are paid off, his goals accomplished, Pa will "retire."
I have moved to part-time, until Social Security. Will not have to move.

1983. February 7.
I smiled at Mother, through hall window, Code blue sounded, she is gone. World's longest umbilical cord severed.

If I cannot do for her, I will not continue attempting to please a new, unstable, female, ex-Army officer - with two recent DUIs, which I discovered too late.

With Golden Handshake, I can resign immediately with eighteen years' credit instead of sixteen, $350 HSU retirement until Social Security.

1988. Meager years. Pa has substituted.
-In high school, girl's gym where he played Jane Fonda aerobic tapes.
-Saturday student disciplinary sessions, cleaning parking lot where he let them open car doors, radios blaring. - attendance swelled.
-Continuing Ed where he destroyed student notes requesting him for permanent teacher.

After volunteer Pink Lady, I work as part-time medical librarian at local hospital, record physicians credits for educational courses on computer, take minutes at physicians meetings.

1990. Now, Social Security! We'll be fine.

1992. Winter: Mid life crisis - didn't know women had them - came during empty nest syndrome period - didn't know it had a name - when I began losing myself and my family. Depression hit hard. Ignorant about that, also, stared at the empty fireplace for two days, much to Pa's frustration. Tore pictures out of the family album, distributed them in four scrapbooks. Already miss them.

Had each child's photograph at age eighteen mounted in one frame, pass them in the hall every day and am relieved of a few regrets.

Spring.
Letter from David to Susan at Cedar Creek:
Since I turned 30, I've noticed certain changes have gradually crept up on me; the fact that Grannies and Grandpas don't last forever, favorite jeans just don't fit anymore and my feet are starting to get these ugly dry, cracked, and flaky-skin-looks to them. I even push around more jowl and neck skin when I shave now!

You've sent me letters that are very precious and valuable to me. I just want you to know that I saturate myself with them and recall them throughout the day.

Thank you and I love you, too!
David

1991. Summer.
An open letter to: Susan, Steven, David, Linda:
The quiet coffee hours I looked forward to are not nearly as enjoyable as I anticipated and now that I may sleep, I cannot.

Some things have changed, others have not. The rooster dishes are still here and I love this house as much as I did when it was new. Mid-century, it is called now. Pa's brass mailbox remains on the front porch, the worse for wear from all his years of polishing. The tiled coffee table with Susan's horse is in Steven's home. We sold the Buick and MG. They each served us for thirty years, brought babies home from hospital, took all away at twenty one to marry. The Buick is in Finland and the MG's new owner entered a cross country race in U.S., thirtieth out of one hundred.

Red Clay Bank is covered with evergreens mature enough to log. The owner was right, we were wrong and he is gone. And when David was home for his twentieth class reunion this year he finally got that little old rock out of the hole in the sidewalk. Then carefully replaced it, I noticed. Bright green moss grows to protect it.

You've all had your adventures on ships, planes, and trains, from the Atlantic to the Pacific, India to Japan, Mexico to Alaska, and always back to this little spot on earth. Except David, who now chooses Paradise, California for the sunshine. He said on his weekly Sunday call that he is "hauling bananas like mad." I thought he was hauling pistachios. "Oh, Ma!" He still doesn't think I get it.

You have made grown up friends of each other. Except for that year the boys did not communicate with each other. What was that all about? What fun it would have been to see Steven carrying David when they found each other at an east coast base, or watch the girls discovering Japan when Linda trained aerobic instructors there and sent for Susan who elbowed their hostess' rice paper wall. Much to Susan's dismay.

It is good you have found reasons for continuing your education. Susan took ten years to finish and Linda who never gives up took twenty five years for her degree. Steven left college before his senior year for a job which offered him training that surpassed anything a degree would have done for him. David now seems interested; maybe respiratory therapy, he thinks.

- The dreamer who seemed hopelessly unorganized is a perfect housekeeper and talented artist, who nurtures animals and family, and gathers us together as often as possible.
- The family conscience, who was too timid to jump off the water tower has shown years of courage as a high climber.
- The one who threatened to dismember the salamander is a kind and loving man who inspires us not to let a disability get us down. We all admit trying to walk with one eye closed the year he lost his in the Coast Guard.
- The one who spent the most time alone while I worked is the most independent, resourceful one of us all, earning her generous nature traveling the world with her sewing machine and bicycle, before settling back home as a phlebotomist.

If I gave you birth, you gave me life; if I taught you anything, you taught me everything.

Love, Ma

1993. Letter to Susan and Paul.
The Thanksgiving celebration at your house was The Best. All of your sacrifice (trailer living, caretaking Granny and Grandpa), in building your own house at Cedar Creek shows in its beauty, splendor, and taste.

Be sure to trash it to the max with living, laughing, and wreck it with contentment.

Merry Kiss Moose, I love you both.

Steven and The Kids,

1994. Letter from Barry.

Dear Fannie B and Richie, My Next Door Mom and Dad,

I am flattered by the invitation from Linda to introduce the following Christmas Letters from your great children. I've been sweating bullets ever since. This is no small matter. Though there are many fun, funny and poignant times to recall, and I'm appreciative of the fact that I was there for a good share of them, I must resist the temptation to talk of them here. I would like to say something about each of you but even a few sentences would turn into an unwelcome obstacle slowing your way to the heart of this project.

I see my Erickson roots in so much of what I consider the best part of me but, here, feel limited to mention only one enduring trait. I always wanted to be one of you guys in the fun, wacky, loving, intellectual, artsy family next door. So early on, the idea galvanized that I wanted to grow up and have my own big family. The Erickson fabric of my childhood has become the salt and fibre of my adult life and I am honored to be such an intimate part of your Christmas this year.

Barry
(Eureka School Teacher)

# What Arlington Way Means to Me
## Susan (46)

It seemed that many Sunday rides during our childhood began or ended with the usual prediction of the future. We were told with a calm but firm resolve that if we didn't clean our rooms, if we didn't finish our chores, if our emotional and physical lives weren't performed in a neat and tidy manner we would surely be like the people who lived on Arlington Way; their dreams neglected and forgotten like the unkempt homes some of them lived in. It was a way our parents had of giving visual stimulation to lessons they wished us to learn.

Our frequent journey back through this part of town was impressive and to this day the mention of the sad little street that existed then will bring grimaces to grown-up faces. Much of what we are comes from those many lessons we learned during childhood and if we were taught to grow and learn each day, which we were, new delights and wisdom would be recorded in our souls for the purpose of creating our own worlds of happiness.

There is something missing from my day when I can't spend a part of it hiking or walking. Pa loved to go and do things whether it was on foot, astride a bicycle, or in a car. Many adventures began with, "Do you want to go?" I would look at him, eyes squinting half asleep, wondering if going would be a mistake.

"Where?"

"No. Do you want to go?"

He would not tell me where we were going and I hated it. But I hated the thought of missing out on adventure more, so I rushed to put my shoes on and always went; in the rain, late or early, it didn't matter. I learned that it was a treat and a job to walk, to bicycle, or take a ride in a car to no where and to discover anything and everything.

Pa's idea of what is fair and right is centered around a moral code that is quite creative whereas Ma possesses a code that is on the straight and narrow. My adventures with Pa began a real connection with the secret world of creative imagination. Ma was always home with the youngest. Once in a while she grabbed me and made sure she told me about the most honest and proper way to behave.

Linda is my anchor. I am a dreamer, something else I learned from those walks in the rain, and when those day dreams keep me from life's process of doing, Linda knocks me over the head with a joke or with a look that makes me face the dragons I am avoiding. She was too young when I was growing up to have much influence but she manages to dog my adulthood with growth by pushing me into doing a lot of stuff I would really rather avoid. I am also a procrastinator. I don't think even God would get things done before Linda. When we were in Japan she made me pack five days before we were to come home so we would not miss our plane. Because she would not let me back in the suitcase, I was hand-washing the clothes I wore that day for the next five days. It is good to have someone around to remind me that life is a continuing journey where new things will be learned and changes can be made, although, I wouldn't want her for a college instructor; she keeps moving up the deadline.

Steven has an artist's flair for turning the seemingly most mundane task into a trip to the light fantastic. What may have been a mere family dinner prepared by most was a feast of gourmet delights when it was prepared by Steven. When retold, he can turn a trip to the market into an adventure of the highways, leaving your spirit visiting places unknown and your hair tangled and tossed because just about everything he does is performed while sitting upon his motorcycle. Your eyes are no longer imagining the sights but actually seeing them.

If there is a God he would call my mom one of his gentle creatures and if we live lives before this one she definitely lived one as a Japanese woman. Her goal is to move through life as silently as possible. If it were not for the raucous energy of her family, the quiet sounds would be the only ones heard. There's nothing like shaking her up; the mischief is hard to resist. Without her way, none of us would know the secret of discovering the hidden treasures. Most people only see the beauty of the blossoms above ground, but she has taught me to cradle the roots of the plant in my hands as I would cradle the flower.

David has taught me how to cope happily with things I cannot change and to find fun in changing the things I can. He was always watching out for me. David never made a big deal of anything unless it was a joke. If I needed money, help with a project, or if I wished to keep a secret, his magic was there. Throughout the challenges of his life he has nurtured a sense of humor that is truly admired. The magic is still there.

It will soon be my little brother's birthday again, and I'll look out my window and ache for the sight of him. I remember the boy speeding up our street and the magic of the neighborhood games. He may be a man but through the eyes of an older sister he looks the same. The pictures come when I dream for the past and soon I can see the glimmer of the boy who would escape from the front door and make us find him for dinner. Or the boy who would hear my pleas when I wanted money for a show. He would pull me into his secret place, empty the Uncle Sam bank so I could be sure to go. Throughout my life he has come and gone with the sweet smell of spring or the smile of a summer's song. When I say goodbye it saddens me to see his figure grow small and dim and then I am comforted to know my life is lovelier because of the presence of him.

Each day I am grateful for the wondrous joy of living knowing that I possess the tools I need to change the things that no longer bring me pleasure. It is up to me, however, to realize that energy used cloud chasing is not particularly conducive to the rigorous energy needed for change. The foundation of my life is strong and I will be comforted all my days by the true richness of my inheritance.

What Arlington Way means to Me
Steven (41)

Arlington Way used to be a row of people who didn't want to. They didn't want to have to do all the things you should; taking care of yourself by taking care of your things. To a boy of nine it was easier to convey the idea of taking care of yourself by using an easy-to-see example of what life looked like when you wouldn't. Arlington Way has done that chore many times for me. However, this sad little image of the row of people who wouldn't, sometimes manifested itself into the impossible task of keeping things, belongings, material matters, in a constant and forever-perfect condition.

Unable to see a compromise, my servants became my masters. The glorious and beautiful sights, on a motorcycle that might wear out, were missed many times.

Compromise: I understand that somewhere in the middle is where God lives.

The center is where there is peace and contentment. Use it, don't forever try to save it. It is a tough place to find for me.

Arlington Way and Biscuit Shoes
By David (39)

As I lie in bed with Nanny's pretty autumn-colored afghan warmly wrapped around me, I constantly fight the uncontrollable blinking of welting eyes and think, "How Stupid This Is." It is just Linda's draft of a bunch of dumb stories jumbled together. But I assure you, it isn't so (I only got this far and tried to read this aloud to see if it was cool enough or if it was right. Now my voice is all cracking apart so shut-up, David.)

Anyhow, when Linda called me in Paradise (in the middle of her degree finals) with the idea, I automatically knew it was a wonderful thing to do and that no matter how it turned out it was going to be terrific. I don't think she and I ever agreed that at a certain age her little sister image of being absolutely ignorant and dumb about life would be deleted. After all, she was smaller and younger and she couldn't possibly ever know anything about anything.

But here's to you, Linda...You have grown to be almost exactly like me in many phenomenal ways, in fact, I like you. Here we are grown ups, or what looks like grown up to little kids, getting slam dunked in life. Hey, you gotta chump knee, I gotta chump eye. How ironic you divorce twice; I divorce twice. So you see, when Ma came to Arcata High in the Battlestar Buick and parked where the seniors stand with Varsity jackets on, I really didn't mean "don't walk next to me." I can now see I meant jump up for a piggy back ride to the car. I think Ma came all the way to school on her lunch hour just to take me and my sick parakeet to the vet and we all know how she dislikes driving. She's such a mom.

I always liked you best because I never felt so terminator-like until some kid, I think it was Stanley or Speedy, spit on you at Jacoby Creek School. I could have pulverized him. Well, I had to do something because you told him, "My brother is going to pound you for that!" So there you have just one small instance that changed my life and my feelings toward you.

No, here's another one. When you, Steven, and I were walking up the creek at Granny's, he kept teasing and teasing you until you were uncontrollably screaming. I ran all the way back to the house and made sure I told Granny that Steven was a mentally retarded spastic and he could be that the rest of his life for all I cared. And when you got your new Honda car and came to visit me at the hospital when I lost my eye and I was teaching you about changing oil, lube jobs, tire wear, log keeping, gas mileage, I looked up from your owner's manual to see you running down the street in a zig zag, yelling WAAAAAA! Did you learn that from Arlington Way?

I liked Susan best, too. What a foreign goddess-like, hippie-thinking, Beautiful Dreamer, boy trouble, under my thumb, paint it black, Dotts Drive In, Jills Drive In, sister she was. When she and Ma sat on the front room rug, feet straight out, lifting their arms up at the same time their right buttcheek and leg going forward about a four inch chug, then left buttcheek, then right again, chug, chug, chug down the hall toward the bathroom... was that suppose to do anything at all? Nineteen sixties aerobics? That stuff never made too much sense to me but Susan was doing it so I knew it had a purpose cuz she was the oldest. I wonder what ever happened to the oil painting I did at her little house up by the college. Yep, plenty of fond memories.

I do know that the distinct feeling of Arlington Way will never ever leave me. That is as solidly planted in my brain as boldly and confidently as Lincoln sits in his cold granite chair. The weekends were most assuredly the wonder years. Saturday chores, from sheets piled in the hall at little Erickson barracks to the dreaded, horrible, never ending, always there, miserable, can't ever finish, sixteen feet high, twenty two acre backyard lawn. Oh, the mow-the-lawn chore! The yellow push mower that was never sharp and always skipped three feet and just pushed the grass over. That back yard had grass from Colleen's doghouse all the way to the quarry! Why the hell did Ma and Pa wait until I was forty one years old to change the shape of the back lawn to the size of a postage stamp? Will ya tell me? I bet I worked on that stupid wet soggy half acre field for three hours just to be called a good gurder.

When all the crying and fussing was said and done, I remember riding my little red fat-tired bike past the Plywood Company and the pressboard box type cottages on Arlington Way and thinking, "Man, they don't even have a lawn." That tattered-shack street hovers over you as an example of not doing it right. What is not doing it right?

1. Not changing from your school clothes to your play clothes.
2. Not coming in after the street lights come on.

3. Not throwing away the pants you pottied in instead of putting them in the bottom drawer!
4. Sneaking out the bedroom window and running around the neighborhood.
5. Going to Flynn's A Go Go after church.
6. Stealing a whole bottle of Old Crow from (Gottam Britt's owner) the old man's carport across the street.
7. Dropping the orthodontist's vacuum cleaner in their wading pool.

These are the kinds of things that made you know just where you were going to live if you keep goofing up.

After Saturday's chores of lawn mowing, sheets from cleaning your room, and always the cupboards in the garage, came Sunday's outing. I think this was the first time I was ever introduced to the stories and sights of the notorious street. One brisk sunny bike ride, Pa, Susan, Barry, Steven and I headed out Bayside Road toward Westwood Village. This route took us to the road where the Georgia Pacific Lumber Company's main office was, next to Dolly Varden Mill. This was always a fun ride because the big sign in front of the office had moveable numbers on it. After seeing that the mill had 2,680,000 accidents in one month, according to the sign when we left, we would head toward the log pond. I remember the skunk smell stench from a small creek that flowed behind Arlington Way. This was my first clue that not only did the place show signs of poverty but being real poor really did stink!

In addition to the sight and smell of that place, I remember asking Pa, "How come they don't take care of their houses?" He shifted his three speed into high gear and said while pedaling away, "Because they goofed up, kid." That incident branded a little bit of goodness into a small boy.

I think I got all the way into High School before I realized Pa really didn't own our Bayside Road. All those words about taxes and government stuff that I heard from Pa made sense to me one day on the way to the

Plaza. "Why don't they fix the damn road, I own it," or "You don't like the way I'm driving, git da hell off my road." That wasn't Pa's road, that was just a road that had a hill on it that made me see how close together I could say Whee, Whee, and not get busted for saying wee wee.

- I am positive there are tons of stories and feelings I could put down here. What I think I'll do is jot down a few ideas (why is the word Idea always capitalized?) And see what I still want to write about.
- I still have the mahogany wing tip shoes (definitely not biscuit shoes) I bought from Barry for $10.00 when I was in eighth grade.
- I remember the raspberry lady's son, how raspy his voice was and the way he ran.-I still have the fishing pole he gave me.
- Steven and I took turns sneaking Susan's Honda scooter out to ride around the block.
- The scary sound of Pa's huge WW11 flight boots on the wood floor.
- Peeking up the mannequins dresses at the old Brizards Store.
- Ma's Cessna plane earring she gave Linda and me when we had our tonsils out.

I am trying to think of where that family saying "get a stick" came from. I think it was the Lake City mosquito net prop. Pa's two-inch thick Guadalcanal sleeping bag, that always leaked feathers, was the first thing set up at camp. His mosquito net was always next and always square. Steven's net was kind of draped over a string, leaving about a foot of headroom, but still more organized than mine. For three days I never quite got my net to have military corners like Pa's. One evening when everyone else was off on a trail, Steven and I took a good long look and discovered Pa had used short sticks to hold each corner of his net, so the only thing we could do was take them. When they came back of course Pa knew what was up. He yelled, "Get your own stick!" I'm sure that is where that stupid family saying came from.

In conclusion, since I have other things to do, I would like to focus on my feelings about how Arlington Way affected my life by saying just don't goof up, and get your own stick!

Arlington Way

Linda (37)

I do not remember Arlington Way. I do not remember driving down that street and actually knowing what it meant. I know Steven told me as we played with our imaginary Chatta that all the gang that were not like us lived there. My earliest memories of the street were not the street itself but what Susan, Steven, and David told me it meant. Susan never talked about it much. I think when she was growing up, civil rights and prejudice were the buzz words and she thought Pa was being a John Bircher for doing that to us after a fun day. I did not care except that it was a game he played that was sort of serious to the other kids but not to me.

I think in the first grade I finally started to realize we did not have as much as the other neighbors in the way of stuff, but I learned from Ma that my stuff was special because it was handmade. When the others just didn't treat their things special that made them like Arlington Way. Steven taught me how unique and individual we were. The only difference in the neighbors and us was that they made more money.

On Saturday mornings we threw all of the sheets in the hall around 10:00 a.m. then I would try to walk through them gracefully in the beauty pageant David set up at the kitchen door with the pancake turner microphone. If I tripped on a pillow case he sang out "Chatta from Arlington Way!" I learned that not trying your hardest was the way to lose. He always let me win and I walked around the front room with a hanger around my waist for my gown.
And a rubber band for a bracelet.

Steven and I got our black bikes out and waxed them with copper cleaner from under the kitchen sink, then for months we rode them with big dried globs of Twinkle on the fenders. As we polished them in the shade and not the sun, he would imagine that those other people let their bikes lay outside and rust. In a low spot in the driveway there was always a puddle. When the bikes were all finished, Steven would see how far the wet track would go after riding through it without smashing into the planter as he turned that corner. He was pretty good. Doing a good job was the most important he said. I learned quality from him. I'm sure he knew not to use the Revere Ware pot cleaner but he knew Pa would kill us if we got into his garage stuff and Ma wouldn't even notice. He let me believe that was what to use and if you didn't keep your bike in good shape it was an Arlington Way bike. We called David's bike that. It meant a way of life to us: Trash versus pride. It had nothing to do with money.

David taught me the social aspect of life. He caught me telling others in school I was adopted from an orphanage where the tooth past was yellow and that I had been born on Arlington Way. I was so ashamed. He said I didn't even know what that street was. Not just where it was. He said I had to earn it. And he proceeded to tell me all he knew. That creative hard-working people do not stay there, do not wear clothes with tears and stains, do not have dirty hair or drive dirty cars. He watched over me closely in grade school and if I did anything embarrassing he stopped what he was doing and told me to stop. Why did I always trust his judgement?

One time I fell off the monkey bars and cut both my knees. I was crying and scared and suddenly somebody grabbed me around my chest and lifted me up. I felt like throwing up and didn't understand why. There was David taking me to the nurse and brushing off the gravel from my bloodied white tights. He was actually hitting it off my knees by flicking his hand back and forth. When we got to the nurse, who was also the secretary, she told him to go to class. "No," he said, "She's my sister...not yours!" With his arm around my shoulder we waited silently for the Buick. Every once in a while he tried to make me laugh. "That was a stupid thing to do, where do you think you live...Arlington Way?"

Susan seemed like a ghost in the family. She had to find her way because she was raised by totally different people than me. She taught me that even the people on Arlington Way were valuable contributors to society and to be tolerant.

When Steven gave me a ride on the bar of his bike going down Lena Avenue fast as he could I was completely engulfed in the thrill and excitement although at the bottom of the hill I was always unceremoniously dumped, but it was fun anyway. It gave me the momentum to follow everyone else and get my own transportation and to follow my liberated, independently-thinking sister who had a scooter. So Steven taught me the importance of independence.

I did not go on many of the long Sunday treks with Pa and when I did it felt like it wasn't the real thing that all the other kids could do while I stayed home with Ma. It was not sad. I loved having her to myself and watching fifties movies, ironing clothes, cooking, sewing, or walking to the store.

My mind starts remembering all sorts of disjointed things like the great Saturday night hamburgers where we each got our own little bag of chips and a Pepsi. The basket plates would be taken down from the top of the fridge and the copper hood Pa installed over the stove sounded like a borate bomber. We made our own with pickle, onion, and tomato slices all over the drainboard, then watched Get Smart TV while Pa took a bath. The comic books afterward were always wet; we would wait and wait to get them, Archie, Donald Duck and Sad Sack.

What I treasure now are the memories of the simple pleasures we had like anticipating dinner, comic books, the Saturday night specials and the Sunday treats. None of us were ever criticized for grades or that we didn't try hard enough. I think Mom was just glad we were normal. Whatever that is. We learned early that our stuff was special. When you said Erickson, it was like the name itself was a secret code. Could you ever trust anyone else to take you camping? What made us think Pa was so perfect at everything and only Ma could sew?

There were troublesome times, not unlike other families, yet they seemed big, then. Every time we went to a school function we knew there would be a "misunderstanding" at home. The night David appeared in Brigadoon, Ma decided to wear a short dress which was too much for Pa to handle, he came out in patterned pants and a checkered jacket, his own fashion statement. Ma unpoofed her hair and changed to a dowdy outfit that made her look like Shagundala. When we piled in the Buick, it was like getting into a big bucket it was so deep and serious. For years I only saw the back of the front seat or the dashboard.

There were barbecues with the neighbor kids on the cedar block patio. Those dumb cedar blocks left over from the shingle mill that we had to dig dandelions from in between with a screw driver. Pouring salt water on them was a joke; they always came back. The umbrella over the picnic table and striped green chairs Ma made from a neighbor's discarded awning.

Then there was Barry. Barry seemed to be a world all in himself. The whole neighborhood was mesmerized when he told spooky stories up on the new neighbors' driveway. With his deep voice he scared us so bad we didn't even want to cross the street to go home. He was the one to start Kick the Can and whenever he came to play...it was real. Barry was such a part of the family it seemed there were five kids. You could just say you were with Barry and it was immediately Kings X. His sisters were just extensions of Ma. It was as if the two houses were connected.

None of us can forget the orange box high in Pa's closet filled with all his treasures. We would get into it after school. Steven was in charge of the mercury in the thick glass bottle with the black top. We poured it on the Heirloom bedspread and watched the little balls gather into one. It made coins look new and turned Ma's gold ring to silver for a while.

Now I know, but the only fear then was that Pa would be displeased. A lot! It was a super heavy box and Steven had to step on the projector and don't break the bulb, its expensive. I know. I had to pay for one I broke.

These memories are jumbled and out of sequence but as I write them down they are all as real as if they happened today. Like the time Pa took us to the airport to see the Borate Bomber. There was a metal fence with circles in it that I was not big enough to climb but could poke my fingers through and see the airplanes. We all had car coats with root beer buttons. We were so proud of Pa's job at the airport and so was he. It was like it was his business.

Now as the days go by Pa has less responsibility and more free time to develop into a whole person. Pa, please never confuse new lack of family responsibility with lack of respect from us. Almost every day each one of your children measure themselves or the projects they complete by your yardstick. If there is any more joy we could have, its seeing what you will grow up to be in your old age and to see the types of things you think are fun. You have had your share of hard times and I wish for you not to create anymore. I remember hiding in the closet when you had your outbursts of fright and frustration when you were raising us and not knowing where the next paycheck was going to go. Sometimes it was for David's broken arm or Steven's ear injury from sliding his motorcycle under the neighbor's log truck, or hospital bouquets for me because of my knee injury. If I have another wish it is that you grow old as proud of yourself as we are. I delight so much in sharing thoughts with you and hearing about "how it was."

Pa, I hope this Christmas you will start a new year with the independence you taught us and the willingness to try new things; realizing that money does not mean as much as the quality of life does. That you take time to do things you want and not wait for Ma. Sometimes the best times are telling those who stayed home. Remember, my Jeep is always ready to go get pine cones or look for Rattlesnake Dick's gold.

Ma, my Christmas wish for you is to age peacefully with no fear and to grow confident in your decisions. We all forget things but it does not mean you have dementia (just don't give Susan any more cards with diseases as sponsors! She thinks you are not telling us something.) That you find an inner connection to the divine and that you live your myths. That you forgive and let go of the things of long ago and not let them tarnish the memories you hold dear. Just say no and know that you don't have to travel if you don't wish to and we will still love you. Your endless energy and enthusiasm is just as valuable and desired as it was when we made missions out of salt dough and cloud maps out of cotton in fourth grade. There is so much more to do and see and create. You are not slipping away, you are gaining wisdom that has nothing to do with a degree. By now you have earned five of those.

And since I am typing all of this I get to say DAVID, TOUCHED YA LAST!

1995. May 19. Fiftieth Anniversary at David's in Paradise
Family dinner at Mongolian Restaurant.
I asked if Pa wanted white rice. "After twenty-five damn years you don't know what I want?" And he did not understand why we laughed so long and loud. He recovers quickly, "Well, it seems like only twenty-five."

The children's signed cards:

- Wishing you a fun day and a healthful next 50 years. Love, Susan and Paul.

- Fifty years - WHEW! I love you. Steven.

- To Ma 'n Pa: Things change so fast and are so fun to deal with. Life for me has been everything I could want!! I love you. David.

- Like Susan says, "May you always live where the red tails fly."
Linda.

1997 Ten day Garden Tour to England. Trip of a lifetime.
With my sister. My first walkabout from home. Seventeen years of
saving brochures paid off. David quickly repaid $3,000 truck loan.
Steven got me a cashmere tam and scarf, Susan and Linda took time
off to take Pa on a rafting trip so I could go!

Letter from a Stranger:

*September, 2001*

*Dear Mr. And Mrs. Erickson,*

*I would like to express our sympathy regarding the loss of your son. Though
we were not involved in the incident in which David lost his life, many of
us were present when David was involved in an accident in the Feather
River Canyon in July.*

*Even though we spent a relatively small amount of time with him at that
time, David touched us all in a manner which we spoke of later that day.
His kindness and integrity were apparent even in a time of tragedy.*

*Though it is not often acknowledged, our personnel and their families often
experience long term emotional effects resulting from tragic scenes like your
son's. So much so, we have dedicated our professional lives to decreasing
these types of incidents.*

*If there is anything we can do to be of service, please do not hesitate to call
me, or Public Affairs.*

*Sincerely,*
*Commander, Highway Department*

Take Me With You

Steven

Often, now, my Brothers go close by me, a taste,
a situation will start their run. I thank them whole heartedly,
so close my imagination could never arrive with such fun.

Often, now, I look and see with
larger eyes. Turned deaf to noise of what wins and what
dies. I give thanks to my Brothers for taking me with
them, to find later, life's wordless gifts thanking me for
taking them.

Often, now, when we know and do what's good
down through the bottom of our hearts; that's when you
take me with you and you with me, and again it starts.

Often now, our growth is
easily seen. Your eyes show such promising dreams, to be
sure and strong from tip to stem. I know now who the
Heroes are, and they are indeed where we find them.

A copy of Steven's devastating sorrow for the loss of his brother is in the
room he and David shared until they left for the Coast Guard. (Steven
states the poem's ending also relates to his growing daughter and son.)

2001
Our son has withdrawn from friends and family. Our daughters are
inconsolable. Two weeks after the news Pa began having grande mal
seizures. David did not say goodbye. Time will not heal. There will
never be closure. I don't want closure. Friends say they know how I feel.
No! They do not. Even I don't know how I feel. Or if any of us will ever
laugh again. Our family can never be put back together again.

2003.

I understand Steven has looked for David on byways they rode together and finally "found" him on one meditative ride.

I have seen David. Susan told me it would happen. He was smiling. I matched my forearms to his, from wrist to elbow, holding on so tight he would still be here, calling his name loudly to the family to wake myself and bring him with me. He only had a small mark on his forehead the girls had told us about. He did not come with me.

Each of us *must* find a pathway to survive the rest of this journey. I wish I could help my children who have lost a part of themselves and Pa who cannot hear his name without tears. How can I help them when I cannot help myself?

2008, August 9
To Susan on her 62nd birthday, from Linda's iPhone

The Perfect Day:

At Cedar Creek, David and I watch Granny put on lotion from the fancy Avon bottle. He calls it Granny Goop time. We all go up to our bedroom in the attic and are startled by a bat that flies in the window and spend several minutes as Erickson's working together to solve the calamity, not really planning, just doing stuff.

Next morning, early, we go down to see what is under the Christmas tree. In our nightgowns I follow you and on the way you suddenly jump in the air and land on Steven's blue airplane, oops.

As it gets light in Nantucket we race on our bikes to see the sunrise, turn around and Pa, not wanting to be left out, jeans over pajamas, is riding like he has E.T. in his basket, racing and skidding behind us then waiting at the top of one of the carriage trails.
We walk our bikes down to David's little house in Paradise and get ready to meet everyone at the restaurant for breakfast - the streams of

sun between the pine trees are warm and hot bugs make that shaving-razor sound.

We kidnap Ma in Sunny Brae on her day off and head for Berry Summit snow to put our feet under the bumper of your blue Volkswagon with the daisy on the back and slide in the snow until she gets sick from our diet of Christmas candy and cocoa.

For lunch we ride back from the great houses in Calistoga. Ma has made lunch and we sit at the table by the pool and eat crab sandwiches.

After lunch we take the horses up through Fickle Hill woods in Arcata where we joust with pampas grass and eat huckleberries high up on stumps. They are sweet but sour and you hand the branches to the horses who jerk them from your hand in perfect rhythm with their walk, swishing past the grasses on the trail.

In the afternoon we take Kayak to get a tet ball at Petco then two hours later we take him to see the orange ball at our childhood deer fort near Red Clay Hill, which he bites and deflates. Then a ride in Grandpa's Model A with white ice cream bars covered in chocolate and Skipper dog and his sister Eleanor in the rumble seat driving over Cedar Creek.

We watch the show with Lippizaners changing leads to music and see the bunnies play with the cats in Fieldbrook. In the evening we take Barney-cat for a walk and he fends off the two dogs with swipes as he jumps across the rocks at the creek.

It is late afternoon and we take Ma to see the Fabrege eggs in San Francisco. She wants to pay with her first credit card. After the long bus ride to Yuron it is another long walk up to the tea field and we listen to an old woman singing as she pounds rice, her voice carrying through the bamboo thicket. On the ferry ride, our feet up on the railing, there is the smell of the salty air of Kagoshima.

For dinner we eat in the back yard in Sunny Brae with Barry, Tom, and Mildred and have barbeque chicken with potato salad, go play kick the can and then off to sleep on the cedar block patio with rugs under us and the collie on our legs.

So, you see, all my life has been The Perfect Day and it has taken this letter to you to realize I have had my share of tears and also the joy of running through David's house one last time with you and Choo Choo, the neighbor's dog he borrowed, to know the pain we will all feel when we say goodbye to Ma and Pa, and the blessed thought that you picked me as your sister to teach me what I know.

Happy 62nd Birthday, Sissy! May this time be filled with what you put there...and more!
Linda

2012. Fall: Letter from Susan
Changes at Cedar Creek:

Ma,
What a nice handwritten letter. I am so glad you told me you and Pa were just not used to some of the changes to Granny and Grandpa's little red house. It was very hard to hear and I so appreciated knowing. I would not like changes to my things either. It is really difficult to make Linda feel at home and entertained so she will bring Pa up, keep Pa's stuff so he will like it, move things so I can make it easier to clean - cleaning two houses takes a lot of organization of space and time - do what I love, which is give you guys the best I can do and afford, and make it comfortable for me to take care of. If I had my greatest wish I would not touch it and you and Pa would come up like you use to. It is an impossible task to please everyone. Happily, we are all different.

Pa, David, and I are the most sentimental about family changes. We would always keep things the same but I have to realize it can't be done. I cried so hard when everyone left that I started to have a panic attack, the fourth in my life and they are very scary, you cannot breathe. Then David put his arms around me and said, "Look at the view, Susan." It helped and that annoying, time-consuming brat of a puppy helped also. My heart is broken because I never know if you will come back. There may not be enough deals with Pa that will convince you, and Pa doesn't like to come unless you are here also.

I simply cannot go across the creek and take care of it without making it comfortable for me. I am doing my best. If I were not also thinking of everyone else, I would change everything. It is too lonely and too sad to keep it exactly the way it was. David is gone forever, Granny and Grandpa are gone, Steven is not there, you are unhappy up here, Pa and Linda only come once in a while, I never know when they will come back, and the house is filled with memories of voices I will never hear again. I walk in the back yard and cry over the plants you will never care for again, stare at the bridges and picnic tables Pa has made, trying not to be sad that he can no longer take care of them and then go into the empty house that is cold and no one will tell me when I can build a fire to warm it up for the next visit. It is awful. So I change something and try to keep it the same.

So now we both have told the truth about how we feel. I either never go in it and the mice and neglect take over or I busy myself with the promise of 'someday.' I am glad and grateful you have told me the house now has new happy memories. I loved hearing that I made that happen.

You and Linda, through a lot of tough love, have taught me to make my life work whether my family is around or not. I have grown to embrace the days I do not see the family and we both know that is a big deal. I would like a family gathering at least once a month but life is good.

Crap! The puppy just grabbed the end of the toilet tissue and ran through the house, like a cartoon. I tried to get him and he ran between my legs and made a race track around the kitchen and through the living room. Life is calling.......must go!
Susan

2013. Fall, at Cedar Creek.
eMail from Susan:

Linda,

A couple of days ago I saw a movie called Beautiful Boy. It was about a mother and father who lost their son because he took a gun and killed a bunch of people in his college and then killed himself. They were grieving over their son while the grieving parents of those who were killed were angry and grieving over their own children.

I thought about the parents of the guy who was driving the truck when David died. Even ten years ago I never thought about them much but was angry when the father tended his garden while we looked at the truck at his house, mangled and torn and the last place David was alive. We were devastated and the father seemed to be going about things like nothing happened. I blamed them for the way their son turned out and I blamed the boy and them for David's death.

The movie helped me understand why they acted the way they did and now realize they lost someone too. They lied about who was driving the truck and their son went along to stay out of trouble. Because of the accident and two earlier DUIs, he was facing prison and stuck forever in a wheel chair. He later died from a drug over-dose. Some say he took the drugs on purpose.

Now, after all these years, that movie came into my life. I started thinking about David and missed him so much. I tried to talk to him and then got depressed and told myself once again that he was really gone forever. I waited for the leaf I always get during autumn. One year it blew into my hand after I asked for it. Another year, one blew right inside the truck in my face and then I stopped asking.

But I did ask David to give me a leaf yesterday and found one perched on top of the post at our gate at Cedar Creek and thought it was simply a coincidence. It was a pretty good one because it was unusual that it would land there and stay. But if it was from him, why on earth doesn't he write something to me if he can move a leaf! This time he is really, really gone.

I took the dog for a walk and found a wrench on the county road almost to the highway, brought it back and gave it to Paul assuming it fell out of his truck, or maybe one of the local utility vehicles.

When I got back from the stables - had a great ride with Dresden - I asked Paul about it and he was puzzled about how I got it and where I found it. We usually notice anything in the road that shines. Pa had not been up to Cedar Creek for weeks. Paul told me to look at the wrench. I took it out into the light and saw etched in his own handwriting DME on both sides. It must have fallen out of Pa's truck—or something. But I found it today and today I had said he was gone forever.

When I lose faith it seems David has always answered me in some way. This time in his own handwriting.

I have also found another special movie. Now I think I know what David could have been up to these past years. He could have been writing that movie about the boy with leaves on his legs, The Odd Life of Timothy Green. He could have directed it and cast himself as the main character. The gift of the movie is special because of the way I found it and the beauty of autumn leaves in the story. One year I asked David, if he was still around, to give me an autumn leaf that was falling way off down the creek. The next moment a leaf landed in the palm of my hand and scooted under my fingers. Every year since then I get one in an unexpected way.

The gift of the movie is about not harboring sorrow but opening your heart to the gift of whatever comes into your life, even if it is only for a moment. Like brothers, sisters, parents, grandparents, special dog and cat friends. It is about never giving up on your dreams; they never let you down, are waiting to be found, and will just land in your hand when your heart is open to receive them. It is really not only about the dreams but the fact that you can find joy because you can dream. The gift is knowledge that so much is possible.

My favorite scenes: Timothy on the front of the bike and rocking out at the family concert.
He said, "There is only so much time. When the leaves go, I go."
Susan

2013. Fall, at Rhody Ranch
eMail from Linda:

Susan,
I am glad to feel that you are coming with me on a different plane of awareness. We look to a brighter spot in our lives when there seems to be muddy waters. The bright spots are indeed in our lives, too. Our memories of David and Steven together are an on-going breathing part of every day when we see a beautiful bird or feel a lovely breeze. It is what we can make of our lives.

Each day, I try to take all the sad stuff and push it to the side and make room to fill my life with freshly cut roses. I keep this time for myself and for my wonderful memories of how sweet Steven was with David and how happy he was when they were together and how silly they played together even as adults. I put that in my coffee every morning, and all of David's love and hugs into the foamy milk. And mom's laughter and Pa catching that lizard yesterday - which by the way was no where near you at all, you big baby - of you riding your horse, of you getting the Golden West speech plaque, of me seeing the Caribbean on my first cruise job, of you joining me in Japan, of us reading Potter's Two Bad Mice in bed. And I get ready for my day.

I push aside all the weedy bad things, sad memories and such, look at the wonderful ones, and the love surrounding me, drink the last

swig of coffee, spit the grounds back in the cup and go for my day.
Each day...
TA, TA, le

Found on Pa's desk:

What are the Bulbs For?
Once upon a time, like a river in flow,
There was excitement, I need you to know.
You couldn't touch it, see it, or hear any sound.
It was there and you'd feel it all around.

Our David is gone now, forever, you see,
So, sad and tearful we'll always be.
Now I look for peace in a place,
A windwayward breeze, a flower, a cloud with a face.
You choose it my friend, he'd want it that way.

So I plant life for spring and I hear him say
I'm doin' stuff Pa, what're you doin' today?

2014 eMail to Pa,
From Susan:
My Perfect Day??
I live at the water's edge in a house made of stone. The sound of my
favorite loon greets his mate and my day. The sleepy dog opens one eye
and his gaze follows me about the room as I open the window to see the
early light glide across the water, then the fields and finally land on the
backs of the horses. The cold flows from their nostrils like the steam
from a train. Soon the rising sun will change from the color of dawn to
the soft blue of it is time to get going.

The large kitchen awaits the humming noise of family and breakfast.
Everyone promises to get up early enough to make me hustle and just
late enough for me to finish some chores in the barn.

There is no need for a watch when you share life with horses; their sense of time is as accurate as Grandpa's pocket watch and you never miss an appointment with a horse and his breakfast. Each horse greets me with his softest nicker, hoping I won't notice how cleverly he has managed to snatch a mouthful of hay from under my arm. I always hope to make them wait until the hay has reached the manger but like many promises of discipline and the animals that share my life they are never kept.

With the horses fed I follow the path from barn to cottage, being careful not to step on the cats weaving in and out my legs. Breakfast wafting from the wood stove begins to visit each room in a symphony of aromas that taunts the sleepiest guest. Soon the people I love and cherish the most will fill my home and the old kitchen table with the sweetest sound I know, the sound of all of us together again.

gMail from Linda to Pa:

I know, Pa. All the pains and aches are so maddening! Even I cry because I cannot do what I use to do. I look in the mirror and turn away; not liking what I see.

When I sit at the pond watching the birds and see David's favorite belted king fisher, I know he is there and am not afraid to leave here, even though it will be forever. We have to think we shall see everyone again.

Remember what he used to say when he was troubled, "I'm gonna' let the Other Me take care of this."

The only thing we have left now is being kind and loving to each other. Steven has missed so many family times and for that I am sorry, but if he ever needs help I will be there and so will Susan.

Things change. I just look at them and try to adjust and keep stress down. We have had a remarkable journey with parents who showed us the way.

Today

Linda's Ice-skidding Accident.

On her steep road home just missing a telephone pole and terrified.

In her inimitable style she informed the family "And don't ask David for any more help today he's too tired from saving ME! He just picked up my car and threw it away from the pole."

# Last Mother's Day

I believe only special souls are destined to leave this earth before their parents, that there is an unexpected blessing in Senior Vagueness, (Google it.) and that anyone who manages to tip toe all the way through the muddy tulips needs to learn the nuisance of good-byeing. I have, and it is. Only a nuisance.

My tears had almost dried up like my laughter gone to powder but today there were stinging drops that dissolved old laughter again, satisfied to be alone, reading between the lines what was not written. Sons and daughters appeared together on the pages, growing taller, older, more loving, and not shy of the word. Susan still says anything Linda does is fine with her, except hum Beautiful Dreamer. Off key. In public. Linda has always declared Susan is more like an angel than anyone she knows, albeit not so Susan hears. Sensitive Steven and sweet-tempered David formed a mutual admiration society in letters and actions and taught grumpy old Pa that not only can men drink three-fingered tea and smell the roses, but they can bear-hug until it hurts and it does not.

For now, everyone is settled in comfortable nests with their spouses all within forty miles of this old house:

Susan hobbys horses and houses, canines and felines, and an organic animal biscuit endeavor, hoping for time to smell oil on canvas again.

Steven begins a new marriage and on holidays they send greetings from the morning side of Berry Summit where there is rest from labor-intensive careers and time to contemplate grown children and grandchildren; two and counting.

Linda, after teaching aerobics in India, Japan, cruise ship hostessing, then a phlebotomist career, in retirement, has produced outdoor figurines and a charmingly illustrated gardener's journal.

And David? He remains in that paradise where sun-tanned summers last as long as he wishes, probably still busy just "doin' stuff" and watching out for all of us. If we lost something he could always find it. We still ask him.

Meanwhile, my mountain of unnecessaries still awaits answers but like the wrathful old man in Steinbeck's grape book, I've decided this is my dirt and I ain't aleavin' it! Nor this old house. Someone I once knew... told Rhett Butler she would think about that tomorrow and so I will, when Pa comes home. *Tomorrow? Did you forget again, old woman?* He will shuffle down the hall calling Ma! because he was not met at the kitchen door.

"You don't care how long I'm gone, do you?" he'll ask and I'll answer, "I still live here, don't I?"

Someone wisely wrote, "The girl is mother to the woman," and it is true. As for you my, long-suffering Younger Self, you taught me so many lessons. You were more competent than you recognized, stronger than you realized, and at last I appreciate your mind and body. Especially your body! *Confucius say*: *For shame, nipples frown down on navel looking up and back is now a question mark.* While we never seduced a king, we did accomplish the worthwhile things and it is my plan to read them this time every year. No regrets. Only gratitude that I have lived to hug all my children as adult friends, listened to their stories, memorized their laughter and did not have to wonder how they would grow up; perfectly normal or vice versa.

Again the day grows chill, dark, and late. I have lowered the sun, rinsed my cup, wound His cat, and fed the clock. The candle has burned down and the oven is closed up, for who needs to heat a whole house to warm half a person, really? And now, may we lay me down to sleep? If I should -

*- Yes, let's! That's NUFFA YOU for today, my dear old crone. When you go, I go.*

05/08/2015

2019.19.2

CPSIA information can be obtained
at www.ICGtesting.com
Printed in the USA
BVHW031510220419
546180BV00001B/60/P

9 781796 023541